W9-BWE-960

Teams
Structure, Process, Culture, and Politics

Eileen K. Aranda

President, Aranda & Associates

Luis Aranda

Arizona State University

with Kristi Conlon

Intel Corporation

Prentice Hall, Upper Saddle River, New Jersey 07458

Acquisitions Editor: *Stephanie Johnson*
Associate Editor: *Shane Gemza*
Editorial Assistant: *DawnMarie Reisner*
Editor-in-Chief: *James Boyd*
Marketing Manager: *Tami Wederbrand*
Production Editor: *Maureen Wilson*
Managing Editor: *Dee Josephson*
Manufacturing Buyer: *Diane Peirano*
Manufacturing Supervisor: *Arnold Vila*
Manufacturing Manager: *Vincent Scelta*
Composition: *Omegatype Typography, Inc.*
Copyeditor: *Nancy Dupree*

 Copyright © 1998 by Prentice-Hall, Inc.
Upper Saddle River, New Jersey 07458

All rights reserved. No part of this book may be reproduced, in any form or by any means, without written permission from the Publisher.

Library of Congress Cataloging-in-Publication Data
Aranda, Eileen K.
    Teams : structure, process, culture, and politics / Eileen K.
Aranda, Luis Aranda ; with Kristi Conlon.
        p.   cm.
    Includes bibliographical references and index.
    ISBN 0-13-494584-0
    1. Teams in the workplace.   I. Aranda, Luis.   II. Conlon, Kristi.
III. Title
HD66.A726   1998
658.4'02—dc21   98-2936
                                                         CIP

Prentice-Hall International (UK) Limited, *London*
Prentice-Hall of Australia Pty. Limited, *Sydney*
Prentice-Hall Canada Inc., *Toronto*
Prentice-Hall Hispanoamericana, S.A., *Mexico*
Prentice-Hall of India Private Limited, *New Delhi*
Prentice-Hall of Japan, Inc., *Tokyo*
Editora Prentice-Hall do Brasil, Ltda., *Rio de Janeiro*

Printed in the United States of America

10 9 8 7 6

Brief Contents

Contents

APPENDIX: INDIVIDUAL TEAM CHARTER 169

Introduction

Throughout history people have worked together to accomplish tasks, make decisions, and solve problems. The purpose of this book is to show how formal teams are able to do more than just accomplish tasks that the individual alone could not. To understand the power of teams, we need to understand that teams are a marriage of structure, process, culture, and politics. These four elements offer a framework on which we can build an understanding of how teams work and how individuals can learn to work effectively in teams.

The framework is dynamic rather than static. Teams are created (structure); then they begin their work (process). As teams work, they form values (culture), and the teams learn to influence (politics). Ongoing assessment (renewal) helps teams to revise their structure; then the whole framework cycle begins again.

Ongoing assessment helps us see whether the team is operating effectively. The five assessment criteria for determining the effectiveness of teams are these:

Quantity of work

Quality of work

Knowledge

Initiative

Collaboration

This text is divided into four parts. Part I deals with issues that arise in the formation of teams and provides tools for defining structure, clarifying the purpose of the team, and the role of leadership. Part II discusses questions that arise as teams develop. Team processes are defined to ensure that progress is made. Processes discussed include the development of team ground rules, participation requirements, and decision-making processes. Part III takes a look at the "anchors" of a team. Anchors and the resulting culture are evidenced in the team's values, rituals, and learning. Part IV deals with more advanced topics, including strategies for effectively implementing the team's work as well as the process of team evaluation and renewal.

How to Use This Book

The activities in this book require readers to reflect on their past experiences with teams. Because of the varying levels of experience, teams may be defined differently in these exercises. Teams as a part of the workplace are the best source to draw upon for examples, because the functioning of teams in the workplace offers the broadest context for the new organization wishing to utilize the team concept. However, in the absence of employment team experiences, nonwork group experiences will serve a similar purpose. Appropriate alternative group settings include the following:

- Civic/community organizations
- Social/service organizations
- Church groups
- College resident halls/sororities/fraternities
- Homeowners associations

Activity: List the teams in which you have participated. This will help you with the reflections exercises in this text.

1.

2.

3.

4.

5.

6.

7.

8.

9.

10.

11.

12.

PART

Defining the Team Structure

Learning from this section:

- To understand the implications for using teams within the organization.

- To be able to differentiate between the types of teams available to organizations and when it is appropriate to use each.

- To be able to identify the criteria for team membership and the roles members play within the team.

- To understand the importance of purpose to team success and know how to define a workable team purpose.

Other things I want to learn about team structure:

-

-

Bringing a new team together offers a unique opportunity to design in an increased likelihood of team success. What the team is charged to do, who comprises the team, and how the team chooses to operate set the stage for, and often the limits of, accomplishment.

In this section we will consider the basic decisions to make and actions to take in the early stages of building a team. We will begin with a discussion on the overall design and structure of the team within the organization. This puts the use of teams in context with other organizational decisions. Then we will look at some specific dimensions of a team including choice of structure, membership criteria, size, skill mix, and need for flexibility. After considering these essentials of team makeup, we will look at the need for establishing team purpose. Without a clear understanding of purpose, with associated goals and measures, the team will have trouble sustaining membership and achieving results. To meet because it has been directed to do so or simply to foster relationships is not enough to drive a team to excellence. Purpose gives the team the desire to learn, the reason to achieve.

Finally, we will look at the role of leadership as it relates to teams. The influence and practices of external and internal leadership impact freedom of process and innovation in team decision making. The leadership approach the team adopts, therefore, has a significant effect on both the efficiency and effectiveness of the team.

Structure

Structure refers to the design and rationale for using teams within the organization. If teams are to be useful to the organization, they cannot be brought into existence haphazardly. Teams are time consuming and challenging to manage, and they need an underlying sense of order and purpose to get started and to perform well. This need for an underlying structure when creating teams becomes more important as organizations look to establish "virtual" and cross-functional teams because the uncertainty and diversity inherent in these teams themselves demand a firm foundation if the team is to reach its potential. Thus, when we talk about the structure for a team, we need to look to two levels: within the organization and within the team.

Teams need to be structured in a way that allows for the benefits of stability and the vitality of change.

We often see organizations creating teams simply for the sake of having teams. The business press is advocating the use of teams; many well-recognized organizations are using teams. As a result, the leaders in other organizations begin to think that they, too, should have teams. Thinking that teams are a "nice touch" or that teams will be a panacea for all organizational ills is a dangerous place to start a teaming process.

Many quality circle teams in the productivity improvement movement of the early 1980s became victims of the "everyone should be on a team" thinking. Teams were created, but often they had little real purpose. The result was that team members became frustrated because no one seemed to care about the *work* the team was doing. Teams became an end unto themselves, but that was not reason enough for them to endure.

The same team fervor is occurring now with Continuous Improvement Teams in the Total Quality Management (TQM) movement. Though most Quality initiatives suggest a Quality Council to oversee teams, they are primarily used to evaluate team proposals, not to determine the value and use of teams in the first place.

Thinking that teams are a "nice touch" or that teams will be a panacea for all organization ills is a dangerous place to start a teaming process.

As a first step, management needs to determine the role for teams within the organization. As we look at teaming within the organization, it seems that top management often wants the results of teams without first engaging in the preliminary design work to develop an organizational structure that uses teams.

To be effective, teams need a direction and purpose that tie into the overall strategy and vision of the organization. Therefore, the initial task in creating teams is for the leaders of the organization to decide how teams should be used in the organization.

For example, an early question management must ask itself is if it is interested in developing an organizational structure based on project teams or process teams. The former usually can operate under the prevailing organizational structure of departments and functions. When management chooses to use project teams as a basis for work design, they usually switch the organizational structure to a matrix which accommodates the complexity of the organization through dual reporting responsibilities. Matrix organizations urge functions to work together on a common goal, but they maintain the traditional hierarchical and functional relationships.

A matrix form of structure is what we often use when we create a task force (see Figure I.1). We bring people together who represent different functions. The responsibility and accountability of team members usually stays with function, and in designat-

Project/Function	Development	Production	Accounting	Logistics	Sales
Desktop Publishing Software	4.5 People assigned	8 People assigned	1 Person assigned	½ Person assigned	1 Person assigned
Accounting Software	3 People assigned	6 People assigned	½ Person assigned	¼ Person assigned	1 Person assigned
Language Software	6 People assigned	4.5 People assigned	1 Person assigned	½ Person assigned	2 People assigned
Graphics Software	9 People assigned	10 People assigned	2.5 People assigned	1 Person assigned	4 People assigned

FIGURE I.1 Sample Matrix Team Structure

ing team members, we often deliberately strive for equal representation of all functions. Designed as such, the team can become an exercise in balancing power, rather than solving a problem or pursuing an opportunity. Below is a typical matrix structure. Each person within a box has dual reporting responsibility—first to function, then to project.

On the other hand, if the organization wants to move to a more radical team arrangement and use *process* teams, there will need to be some fundamental structural changes in the organization (see Figure I.2). Process teams give up their departmental boundaries and loyalties for commitment to the overall process. This may ultimately mean disbanding the department in favor of creating permanent multi-functional units around key processes. This kind of reorganization challenges the power and reporting

FIGURE I.2 Sample Process Team Structure

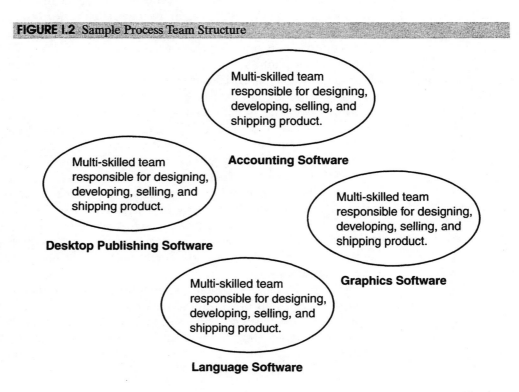

Multi-skilled team responsible for designing, developing, selling, and shipping product.

Accounting Software

Multi-skilled team responsible for designing, developing, selling, and shipping product.

Desktop Publishing Software

Multi-skilled team responsible for designing, developing, selling, and shipping product.

Graphics Software

Multi-skilled team responsible for designing, developing, selling, and shipping product.

Language Software

relationships within the organization, and management needs to consider the implications of this level of change before succumbing to the promises for performance indicated with process teams.

Many organizations wistfully hope to change how they do business without really changing how they do business. As depicted above, process teams do not fall easily into the natural hierarchical structure. It is not clear who is in charge and what the reporting relationships are. Within the team, functional roles become fuzzy if not totally abandoned. The team operates more like a small business—everyone doing what needs to be done and not being too concerned about job title. A good example of this kind of structure is the GM Saturn plant. Teams have eliminated most job titles, are heavily cross-trained, and see their goals as belonging to everyone on the team. Process teams can be very powerful but they require a fundamental change in organizational structure to work.

> Just as with a "robust" product, teams need to be able to be "dropped" several times and still work.

Overall structural decisions usually lead to another question for organizational leaders to ask. Do they wish to direct the teams through an external source of control (a manager or team leader), or do they want to create self-led teams? There has been much advocacy for self-led teams and they can bring great benefits to the organization. But, there is a structural price to pay for such a team design.

Bringing teams into existence under the traditional command and control structure with a manager "in charge" is easiest, and in fact, will look like and result in the committee structure many organizations have now. Historically, the concept of teaming has been easiest to embrace at the top and bottom of the organization. That is, the people at the top think it is a good idea for the people at the bottom to work together in teams. But it is the people in the middle who must make this structure work. "Supervisors" at all levels must buy into the team design and learn new skills.

For teams to work under a chain-of-command structure, managers must be willing to fundamentally change their behaviors. This behavior change in the organization is usually defined as moving from a directing role to a coaching role. Much has been written about the value of this change in managerial behavior, but in practice it is difficult to achieve.

Using teams as an integrating mechanism within the traditional hierarchy is a workable model, but it requires a great deal of explaining, advocating, developing, and rewarding within managerial ranks to make it work. If teams are tightly controlled by management, they will not realize the potential of their collective thinking. They will simply reflect the ideas and preferences of the supervisor or manager. If the direction of the manager is too strong, utilizing a team is a waste of time and energy. You could get the same results in much less time if you just let the manager make the decisions.

To create teams with the ability to self-manage requires a very different structural model. Self-management does not mean that teams take over the organization, but it does mean that there must be an organizational power shift downward into the team. Self-led teams often take on many formerly supervisory tasks, including purchasing materials, managing inventory, assigning schedules, and even selection, evaluation, and compensation of team members. This gives the organization the opportunity to remove a level of management, or perhaps more wisely, gives supervisors more strategic, integrative roles to play.

The team does not take on these supervisory tasks without initial training nor continued guidance. Many organizations have declared teams to be self-managed and have removed supervisory support only to see them founder under these new responsibilities. In the same way that managers need to be trained and developed under a team structure within the current hierarchy, so self-led teams need to be trained if they are to be the new structure.

Hierarchically Driven Teams				Self-Directed Teams
1	2	3	4	5
Specific tasks and methodology defined by management; team membership based on balance of power.		Some ability to define task and methodology, but permission-driven. Team members interested in preserving position of the functions they represent.	Vision and desired outcome provided by management; strategy and tasks decided by team. Members' primary concern is achievement; accountability is to the team.	

FIGURE I.3 Structure Control Continuum

Organizations do not need to choose between chain-of-command-oriented teams and self-led teams. Rather, these two choices are at opposite ends of a continuum of control for teams (see Figure I.3).

Management must decide where on the continuum they ultimately want to be and how long they are willing to take to get there. The further down the continuum and the faster the time frame, the more fundamental and radical structural change needs to be.

As you can see, the decision to create teams in the organization is not without consequence. If the organization is serious about using teams, it needs to think carefully about the implications they will bring to the power and structure of the organization. These structural decisions are fundamental and are precursors to making the choices described in the three chapters in this section. If the tactical decisions in the following chapters are made without a strategic intent for the team structure, team performance will be highly stressful and success will require extraordinary effort. Organizations do not want to put teams in this situation. To make it easy for them to succeed, management needs to create an important, credible, and supported role for teams in the organization.

Background Reading

Many of the concepts in this section are supported by research and other writings. Some of the key foundation work is included in the materials below. If you want to expand your knowledge of teams and structure, please explore this information.

Katzenbach, J. R. and D. K. Smith. 1993. *The Wisdom of Teams.* Boston, MA: Harvard Business School Press. An important discussion on the characteristics of successful teams the authors observed in the workplace.

Kinlaw, Dennis C. 1991. *Developing Superior Work Teams.* Lexington, MA: Lexington Books. An excellent presentation on the technical requirements for building teams in a total quality environment.

Orsburn, J. D., L. Moran, E. Musselwhite, and J. H. Zenger. 1990. *Self Directed Work Teams.* Homewood, IL: Business One Irwin. For more information on the development and functioning of self-directed teams.

CHAPTER

Team Essentials

Learning from this chapter:

■ To be able to compare and contrast the types of teams that operate in the organization and how to address the unique needs of each.

■ To understand the criteria for effective membership in a team.

■ To understand the skill mix needed to have a competent team.

■ To explain and add flexibility to team structure.

Other things I want to learn about the essentials of putting a team together:

■

■

Once top management in the organization has addressed how teams can enhance organizational performance and has defined the specific expectations for teams within the organization/unit, there are some basic guidelines to follow for bringing teams together and starting them off on the right foot. Just as using teams in the organization cannot be a haphazard process, neither can the creation of the individual team. In this chapter we will look at some of the basic choices in design that organizations have when creating teams.

Types of Teams

There are three general kinds of teams that organizations use:

Work teams:	teams that form natural work units, doing the day-to-day work of the organization
Task teams:	teams that address a specific problem or opportunity
Management teams:	teams drawn from people who direct operational or organizational units

Each type of team has an appropriate application and specific requirements and issues to consider. Membership, skill development, stability needs, and overall implications for the use of teams in the organization need to drive the team design decision. Care must be taken at this early point in the team's life to enhance its chances of success.

WORK TEAMS

Natural work groups are the most logical teams to create within the organization. These teams might come from existing organizational units such as sections or departments, or they might be regional units such as small field offices. While they are the most natural of teams in the organization, these units have normally worked as a collection of individuals rather than as a team. Frequently, work unit members do not visualize or share a common goal for the unit; seldom are they rewarded for unit performance. On the other hand, these groups often perform common, interdependent work, and so it often makes sense for organizations to start a team initiative with work teams.

In considering a current department or function as a likely base for a work team, important changes taking place in organizational structure need to be considered so that appropriate work teams are chosen. Across industries increasing emphasis is on creating cross-functional or process teams. When deciding how to develop work teams, one of the most important concerns is who should be part of the work team. The organization needs to have a clear view of its desired long-term structure as it brings teams on as common organizational units. For example, if the organization is working toward cross-functional and process teams, it needs to be cautious about encouraging unnecessary cohesion among functional groups.

> It is very important for management to put the creation of a team in context; to consider how this team will impede or reinforce management's desire for the evolution of the overall organization's structure.

A concrete example of a situation where an organization had to choose the type of work team it wanted might be helpful to elaborate this point. An organization wanted to improve its order processing and delivery performance. Order processing in the organization was traditionally structured with departments for order entry, credit, packaging, inspection, and shipping. Each function was responsible for managing its particular issues for all of the company's customers.

As the company grew it added more people to each department to handle the work. As is typical, each department developed procedures that suited its needs, drew boundaries around its responsibilities, and focused on internal issues and efficiencies. The larger the departments became, the less they knew what the people were doing in their units and in related units, and the easier it was for things to be left undone. Customers became increasingly dissatisfied because they were never able to talk to the same customer service person twice; each phone call required telling the employee the history of the account. Customers also were often given inaccurate information because information was not easily shared within the department. In addition, since order processing consisted of several steps involving different departments, customer files could be unavailable, out of the department that needed them when a call came in. The employee could not know the current state of the order. As a result, customers were constantly being transferred from department to department in an effort to locate their orders.

As a response to customer complaints, the company decided the customer would be better served if the employees worked together better. The company decided to create teams. But what kind of team did it want to create? There were at least three choices:

1. *Create teams for each department.* That is, establish an order entry team, a credit team, a packaging team, an inspection team, and a shipping team. Have each of the groups learn to work together and share information within the team.

2. ***Build a team for the entire order processing function.*** That is, create a team which would bring together all the employees from the different departments currently involved in order processing.

3. ***Build a team for the entire delivery process.*** This team would include people within the company, but outside the traditional order processing departments, who had great influence on the delivery process, specifically accounting and manufacturing.

The issue here is not that the company make the **correct** choice. None of the choices is intrinsically right or wrong. However, each has tradeoffs. The key to a wise decision is defining how the teams fit within the larger organizational structure and how they can function best.

If the choice is to build the teams within the current departments (choice 1 above) it will be relatively easy to get some quick efficiency improvements. Each person knows the work of the department and can probably offer good suggestions for improving the way work is done. However, in the long term this may not help the customer. Each unit may work better and still neither speed up the overall process nor necessarily provide the customer with better information on the current state of an order—all because the team is not cross-functional.

If the choice is to build a cross-functional team of the current order processing department (choice 2 above), teamwork will be more difficult. The members of the cross-functional team will not readily understand the work of the other departments. It is even possible that the different departments have been blaming one another for the current problems and that team members therefore will be defensive about suggestions to change their part of the process. Such teams traditionally take longer to establish and in the process will change the way the company does business.

> To be effective, teams need to be small enough to allow people to develop relationships, to provide for participation at meetings, and to engender a feeling of mutual accountability.

Also, the number of people included in this team will be too large. This may be the case in the first choice as well since the departments are getting larger and larger.

In the next section we will discuss more about the appropriate size of teams. Suffice it to say at this point that a team made up of all the departments would somehow have to be broken down into smaller subgroups.

The up side of the cross-functional team choice is that the customer is likely to see improvement. Working together, the entire order process can be improved. Since the general work of the unit is relatively similar, there would also be the opportunity for cross-training, thus enhancing the overall capability of the team.

The choice to bring together an overall process team (choice 3 above) would be the most challenging to achieve. The team would now have people who speak different organizational languages, do different kinds of work, and may have conflicting performance goals. Not only will this team take more time to understand each other's views and values, it will require the organization to share information at a new level and to break down its assumptions about separation of tasks and control. For example, management would have to decide to whom this team would be accountable and what decisions the team could make.

> Without a deliberate effort to manage the different points of view represented on the team, those differing perspectives will likely lead only to conflict.

However, if this team can perform well, the customer will likely receive the most benefit because this team can deal with effectiveness (doing the right things), as well as efficiency (doing things right). The first two teams are limited to dealing primarily with efficiency issues.

Thus, the critical first step in developing teams is to understand the impact of the team on the organization. If the company makes choice 1, the organizational structure can stay the same; improvement occurs within the current unit. Choice 2 requires the organizational structure and reporting relationships to change somewhat. People are brought together differently, necessitating adjustments in supervision and management, though the nature of the work stays the same. Choice 3 not only changes the reporting relationships, but brings people together with entirely different responsibilities and goals for the organization. Choice 3 requires a radical change in organizational power and decision making.

The organization described in the example above selected choice 2. It designated subgroups around account size and region. Since the organization had a very traditional structure and very conservative management style, combining similar functions was seen as enough of an initial change. Once those teams are working well, however, management might be encouraged to spread the lateral interaction and responsibility further. Management must put the creation of a team in context to consider how this team will impede or reinforce management's desire for the evolution of the overall organization's structure.

TASK TEAMS

Because they are by definition temporary, task teams do not present the same structural problems found in work teams. With a task team there is no sense that the team needs a different organizational structure to manage it. However, since task teams are often among the first teams brought into the organization, it is wise for management to consider all the implications of bringing them on board. Task teams are not without problems—two of the most important being valuing other perspectives and managing implementation.

Task teams are usually cross-functional. The whole idea of the team is to get as many different ideas about a given problem or opportunity as possible. But we often think that just bringing the group together is enough to benefit from its heterogeneous membership. Experience has taught us otherwise.

Let's look at a common scenario for a task team. The organization wishes to draw together representatives from different departments to solve a problem. In this case, the organization is relocating and a team has been charged with deciding on the layout and design of the internal space, selection of new furniture and accessories, and the location of people and equipment in the new building. Without a deliberate effort to manage the different points of view represented on the team, those differing perspectives will likely lead only to conflict. Each person will feel that it is his/her responsibility on the team to be an advocate for his/her own department and protect its interests. Successful membership on the team will be viewed as getting the "best" for one's constituency. With this view, the team is off on a downhill slope, for there is no sense of common goal for the team nor common good for the organization, and therefore, no way for everyone to feel successful.

As the organization brings a task team together, it must carefully design the team so it can work together. Some of the design issues to address are:

1. *Power level and mix of people in the team.*   The more implementation-oriented the task, the more levels needed.
2. *Disposition of members toward problem solving and collaboration.*   The more controversial and the greater the time pressure, the more important to have able problem solvers on the team.
3. *The amount of time allowed to address the issue.*   The more innovative (requiring thinking outside current mindsets), the more dedicated blocks of time are needed.
4. *Specificity of task.*   The more controversial and/or strategic, the more the desired outcome needs to be well defined.

For example, one design decision might be how to balance the position power in the team; that is, should team members all come from the same level of the organization so that "bosses" in the group do not pressure "subordinates" to see things their way? Or, should management spread the levels represented on the team to get multiple views? This mixed-level design is useful if the organization wants to foster communication and respect at all levels of the organization. Techniques that encourage participation and minimize power need to be part of the mixed-level team process.

Often we think that just bringing the group together is enough to benefit from its heterogeneous membership. Experience has taught us otherwise.

Another design decision might be how to put people on the team who are known for their ability to reach agreement rather than people known for stubbornness. A task team needs multiple perspectives to realize its potential, but it does not need people who are unable to learn or to see the value in another point of view. Rather than choosing team members on the basis of extent of specific knowledge, it might be better to base the membership on understanding of the overall implications of the team task or on long-term organizational needs.

The point of this discussion is that, because task teams are brought together expressly to resolve issues, it is necessary to consciously design the team in terms of membership, time commitment, and direction to better be able to work together. Organizations seldom think about the problem-solving approaches and people needed on the task team for it to be successful. They assign people simply on the basis of proximity or availability.

Once the team begins to work together, another problem for the task team can arise. The more the team builds cohesiveness, the less it looks outside its group for input. Therefore, acceptance of its ideas is usually a serious issue for a task team to address.

Take the building design team we discussed earlier as an example. Once the team begins to work together, it will need to resolve issues and begin to make decisions. The more team members are able to come to agreement, the less likely they will be to get information from outside the group. The building task force is likely to get very involved in its task, to develop cohesive relationships, and to spend a lot of time together. The organization will assume the team effort is working well because the team is getting along well together and making progress.

Then, when the "solution" is presented by this "effective team" to the entire organization, it is met with resistance. The team members and management are surprised and annoyed that the rest of the employees do not like the team recommendation, nor appreciate the team's effort. The problem is not that the solution is a poor one, for teams seldom come up with irresponsible or silly solutions, but rather that those outside the team had increasingly little input into the decision. The rest of the employees feel that they are being sold a "bill of goods," and they are suspicious. In fact, the task force often makes the situation worse because it begins the problem-solving process by getting information from its constituents and making promises about future contact. The expectation for sharing information has been set, but as time goes on and the team gets more comfortable with one another, there is less interaction with those outside the team.

The first response of those left out of the process is to argue with the solution and pick out its shortcomings. Since no solution is perfect, there are always plenty of things to argue about. Team members defend their recommendation, get angry at their fellow employees, and say they will never represent the department again. Management decides that teams do not work and resorts to individual decision making.

To get good ideas from a team is not the same as having those good ideas accepted by the rest of the organization. Later in the book we will discuss how to improve the chances of getting good ideas from the team and how to get those ideas accepted.

MANAGEMENT TEAMS

Perhaps the most difficult teams to develop are management teams because they have the least obvious purpose. Work teams usually have goals and objectives or fairly well-defined "work to be done." Task teams are created for a given purpose, though that purpose needs to be important and well defined. But management teams are often not sure why they meet together as a team.

A management team will often say that its goals are those of the organization. But organizational goals are not the same as the management team's goals. Organizational goals relate to the functional responsibilities that the members of the management team have and are focused downward in the organization. Those goals are more closely tied to the manager's relationship with his/her work team than to colleagues on the management team.

A management team needs its own goals defining what it will hold itself collectively responsible for. There needs to be a value-added dimension to the management team itself. The management team often says the value added is improved communication about organizational issues. To that end, the management team has staff meetings where members report on the work/problems/achievements in their departments, and the team sometimes makes operational decisions affecting those departments.

While information sharing may be a useful process, it does not constitute a substantive goal that can bring management together as a team, nor does it result in an achievement that adds value to the organization. Katzenbach and Smith, in *The Wisdom of Teams,* found that simply to report and make occasional operations-level decisions is not an engaging enough purpose to form a team. The level of most staff meeting discussion tends to keep the team members deeply entrenched in their individual responsibility and not focused on the overall good of the organization. The real purpose of a management team is to provide synthesis to organizational goals and activities. Team members must leave their functional identities at the door and deal with the organization as a whole if they are to develop into a team.

Katzenbach and Smith also found that to become a team, management groups must do real work together. Real work for management teams revolves around development of the entire organization. We are learning from organizational studies, especially those in the area of Total Quality Management and reengineering, that viewing the organization as a collection of separate parts is ineffective. Even if all the parts run well individually, the organization will not run well if the units are not integrated. In fact, the better each separate unit runs, the less well the entire organization runs because each unit will optimize at the expense of the others.

Thus, management teams must take on tasks that inspire and integrate the work of the organization. This work usually comes in the form of building a vision, refining the culture, carrying out major change initiatives, or improving the morale/image of the organization or unit. These are tasks that go beyond reporting and deciding functional/operational issues. They require management teams to understand the organization's vision and each other, to set aside their functional views, and to work together on a common purpose. As Peter Senge states in *The Fifth Discipline,* a major obstacle to team learning and good collective thinking is the attitude that "I am my position." This is an especially serious disability for a management team.

In summary, then, there are three different kinds of teams that the organization can use: work teams, task teams, and management teams. Often the organization uses all three. Each of the three kinds of teams has very different needs and implications; and if the organization is going to develop effective teams, it must address the differences within and among these teams. It is not enough just to bring people together or to treat all teams the same.

Characteristics	Work Team			Task Team			Management Team		
Mix of levels of functional responsibility	Rating: Good	OK	Poor	Rating: Good	OK	Poor	Rating: Good	OK	Poor
	Comments:			Comments:			Comments:		
Ability to balance power within the team	Rating: Good	OK	Poor	Rating: Good	OK	Poor	Rating: Good	OK	Poor
	Comments:			Comments:			Comments:		
Attitude toward problem solving vs. protecting turf	Rating: Good	OK	Poor	Rating: Good	OK	Poor	Rating: Good	OK	Poor
	Comments:			Comments:			Comments:		
Reasonableness of time allocation for addressing issues	Rating: Good	OK	Poor	Rating: Good	OK	Poor	Rating: Good	OK	Poor
	Comments:			Comments:			Comments:		
Input gathered from those outside the team	Rating: Good	OK	Poor	Rating: Good	OK	Poor	Rating: Good	OK	Poor
	Comments:			Comments:			Comments:		
Overall effectiveness of team									
Key improvements for team to make									

Reflection

Think about your past membership in the different types of teams. Identify, rate, and then comment on the effectiveness of the design for each team.

Team Characteristic	Work Team	Task Team	Management Team
Power Equalization			
Functional Mix			
Problem-solving Abilities			
Time Allocation			
Outside Input			

Team Work

Given your experience with past teams, now turn your focus to your current team(s). What structural changes would you make to enhance your current team's effectiveness?

Team Charter

Record your suggestions, ideas, and decisions in the Team Charter in the appendix of the book.

Team Size

Through our experiences in the industrial age we have learned that bigger is not always better. People cannot relate to large numbers of people, and they often get lost in the impersonality of big organizations. Throughout all business sectors, we now see large organizations beginning to form smaller groups to gain the focus, energy, relationships, and communication found in small companies.

This same issue of size holds true for teams. To be effective, teams need to be small enough to allow people to develop relationships, to provide for participation at meetings, and to engender a feeling of mutual accountability. If the team is too large, members tend to see themselves as having little impact on team outcomes. They feel that it does not matter if they come to the meetings, nor that their particular skills are needed. Or, they may think that the large size of the team makes the process too time consuming or stressful as members vie for air time and recognition.

There are no absolutes for team size, but experience and research have shown that the most effective team size ranges from 4 to 12 people. With fewer than 4 people, a team lacks perspective. For a complex situation 4 is probably not adequate, though 4 people may form the core of the team. As team membership grows beyond 12 people, it becomes difficult to manage the relationships within the team. Team members break off during meetings and form smaller subgroups. Side conversations predominate, and the group loses focus. Air time also becomes a problem as the team size grows.

Even with only 12 people, each person can speak less than 10 minutes if team meetings last no more than two hours. And, in general, two hours is the maximum a team can meet on a regular basis. After two hours, team members are usually physically tired and intellectually spent. Of course, the reality is that some people speak more than 10 minutes and others speak very little or not at all. The larger the group, the wider the participation gap becomes, and with that, useful communication grows more difficult.

Reflection

Consider two team situations you have been in—one with a large team (12 or more people) and one with a small team (4 or fewer). Now think about the impact of size on team effectiveness.

SMALL TEAM:

Advantages: _____
_____

Disadvantages: _____
_____

How did the team cope with disadvantages? _____
_____

LARGE TEAM:

Advantages: _____
_____

Disadvantages: _____
_____

How did the team cope with disadvantages? _____
_____

Team Work

Now consider your current team. What advantages or limitations are there to its current size?

How can you:

Capitalize on the team's size advantages? _____
_____
_____
_____

Offset the team's size disadvantages? _____
_____
_____
_____

Team Charter

Record your ideas, suggestions, and decisions in the Team Charter in the appendix of the book.

Team Membership

Perhaps the most important decision we make in initiating teams is how we determine the composition of team membership. We often choose team members on the basis of proximity or position, neither of which innately adds strength to the team. A proximity error occurs when we use criteria like seniority, association, or location as the basis for membership. A consequence of such selection criteria is that teams routinely have the same people on them. This results in having those same people using the same perspectives, coming up with the same ideas, and suggesting the same resolutions.

Teams provide us a fine opportunity to bring people with disparate views together and we need to maximize that potential.

Membership based on proximity also often causes or exacerbates divisions within the organization. For example, the home office usually has more representation on a team because they are close together and do not have to travel. This deprives the home office of views from the field and keeps the field personnel from developing positive relationships with those in the home office. Suspicion, indifference, and sometimes hostility are common feelings across field office and home office boundaries. How teams are put together creates or intensifies these feelings. Teams provide a fine opportunity to bring people with disparate views together to build relationships and develop workable resolutions to problems. We need to maximize that potential in teams by carefully defining team membership.

dispévet

Position is another composition decision we make when putting a team together. We tend to put people from the same levels in the organization together on the team. Again, this limits our perspective. The rationale often used for this composition error is that people are more free to talk when they are at the same level. They may be more free to talk, but have we lessened the value of their conversation? Information from above and below the level of team members is usually vital to the acceptance of the decisions it will make. In addition, the active participation of a senior-level team member often gives credence to the work of the team. Inclusion of subordinates in the team gives important perspectives and provides an opportunity for development of the subordinate team member. If there are power problems within teams comprised of various levels in the organization, we need to learn the process and participation skills necessary to work effectively together. Senior people can learn not to intimidate and dominate in a group, and less-senior people can learn to speak their minds and develop new skills. If we do not learn these skills, teams will only perpetuate a shortcoming of hierarchy and reinforce the suspicion between levels in the organization.

The most important aspect of deciding team composition, then, is to look for *contribution* to the team purpose rather than convenience of meeting or balance of power. As team members are chosen, the key questions to ask are:

- What different kinds of information does the team need to work effectively? *Who can provide that information?*
- What skills does the team need? *Who can bring these skills to the team or who is willing to develop them?*
- What cross-functional bridges can be built with this team? *Who needs to be on the team to make this happen?*
- How can the team be a learning/development tool for members? *Who can facilitate this learning on the team?*
- How can the team build relationships among people who do not often work together? *Who should be included in the team from outside the usual membership pool?*

Membership Decisions	*An Example of a Good Design Decision*	*An Example of an Ineffective Design Decision*
Choose people who understand the needs of the organization		
Utilize senior people in the organization		
Utilize less-senior people in the organization		
Bring needed information into the team		
Bring necessary skills into the team		
Achieve cross-functional representation		
Develop relationships outside unit		

Reflection

Think about an organization you are familiar with that commonly uses teams. Based on the criteria given below, evaluate how effective they are in putting teams together.

Team Work

Now, consider your current team or a team you are about to come together with.

What common membership errors exist, or are likely to occur, with this current or new team?

_____   _____
_____   _____
_____   _____

How could you avoid or offset these errors? _____
_____

Team Charter

Record your ideas, suggestions, and decisions in the Team Charter in the appendix of the book.

Skill Mix of the Team

One of the criteria for choosing team members should be the skill needed to address the team's task. There are three kinds of skills that teams need to have: problem-solving skills, interpersonal skills, and task-related skills. Problem-solving skills assure that team members know how to define and address problems and to reach wise decisions. This means the team must know how to engage in dialogue, generate alternatives, analyze options, consider implementation issues, and finally come to a decision on a path to follow. These problem-solving skills will be discussed more in the section on decision making and with the culture information on creativity. Suffice it to say that the team needs to be able to develop resolutions for the issues it was chartered to consider.

Examples of the problem-solving skills that team members need to possess are:

Thinking:	the ability to conceptualize issues
Creativity:	the ability to generate options
Discussion:	the ability to pursue a discovery process
Decisiveness:	the ability to formulate and explain decisions
Implementation:	the ability to follow through with plans and details

The team also needs interpersonal skills. Working jointly on problems is often not an easy nor a familiar task. Someone on the team must be skilled at drawing out information from team members and providing a sense of affiliation among the team members. Some of the needed interpersonal skills can initially be provided by a facilitator. However, these are important process skills that the team itself must eventually develop.

Examples of interpersonal skills to seek out or develop in team members include:

Facilitation:	the ability to keep the discussion focused and moving
Influencing:	the ability to rephrase proposals to meet team member needs
Listening:	the ability to capture the essence of ideas
Support:	the ability to draw out ideas from others
Visioning:	the ability to carry team members through the valleys of the decision-making process

Technical skill is also a key ingredient for team success. The team must have a basis for understanding the issue presented to it. Some members of the team must have substantive knowledge, access to detailed information about the issue, and experience to put the current issue in context. Skills that relate to accomplishing tasks include:

Discovery:	the ability to search out needed information
Organization:	the ability to collect and present information in a useful manner
Analysis:	the ability to interpret information
Synthesis:	the ability to combine information for complete meaning and to prioritize issues
Clarification:	the ability to differentiate between key and secondary information

Learning together is an excellent way for team members to build cohesion and trust.

When choosing members for a team, it is important to focus on the potential development of a skill mix, not just the current state of the team's skill mix. That is, team members must be *willing* and *able* to learn the problem-solving, interpersonal, and technical skills and information needed for the team to succeed. If the organization requires all team members to have all of these skills as a prerequisite for team assignment, the same team members will be assigned over and over again, and the organization will fail to develop new team members.

Learning together is an excellent way for team members to build cohesion and trust. As long as the team has sufficient ability to identify what it wants to learn, a minimal skill level is adequate. One of the indicators of a successful team is that each person is personally and professionally more skilled as a result of the team experience. Every team member should leave with more skills than he or she brought to the table. Again, if team membership is only open to the most skilled, there will be little room for growth within the team.

The team must decide which skills are broad and important enough for it to acquire for both team and personal development and which skills the team simply needs to access.

Reflection

Reflect on your experience in working on a team that was given a challenging task. Using the assessment tool below, evaluate the team's skill. For each skill, first indicate how important that skill was to accomplishing the team's task. Then indicate how well that skill was developed within the team.

Team Skills Gap Analysis

Skill	Skill Ranking — Importance to Task	Skill Rating — Ability for Team to Use
Thinking	1 2 3 4 5 6 7 8 9 10 — None Somewhat Very	1 2 3 4 5 6 7 8 9 10 — Unable Some Skill Proficient
Creativity	1 2 3 4 5 6 7 8 9 10 — None Somewhat Very	1 2 3 4 5 6 7 8 9 10 — Unable Some Skill Proficient
Discussion	1 2 3 4 5 6 7 8 9 10 — None Somewhat Very	1 2 3 4 5 6 7 8 9 10 — Unable Some Skill Proficient
Decisiveness	1 2 3 4 5 6 7 8 9 10 — None Somewhat Very	1 2 3 4 5 6 7 8 9 10 — Unable Some Skill Proficient
Implementation	1 2 3 4 5 6 7 8 9 10 — None Somewhat Very	1 2 3 4 5 6 7 8 9 10 — Unable Some Skill Proficient
Facilitation	1 2 3 4 5 6 7 8 9 10 — None Somewhat Very	1 2 3 4 5 6 7 8 9 10 — Unable Some Skill Proficient
Influencing	1 2 3 4 5 6 7 8 9 10 — None Somewhat Very	1 2 3 4 5 6 7 8 9 10 — Unable Some Skill Proficient
Listening	1 2 3 4 5 6 7 8 9 10 — None Somewhat Very	1 2 3 4 5 6 7 8 9 10 — Unable Some Skill Proficient
Support	1 2 3 4 5 6 7 8 9 10 — None Somewhat Very	1 2 3 4 5 6 7 8 9 10 — Unable Some Skill Proficient
Visioning	1 2 3 4 5 6 7 8 9 10 — None Somewhat Very	1 2 3 4 5 6 7 8 9 10 — Unable Some Skill Proficient
Discovery	1 2 3 4 5 6 7 8 9 10 — None Somewhat Very	1 2 3 4 5 6 7 8 9 10 — Unable Some Skill Proficient
Organization	1 2 3 4 5 6 7 8 9 10 — None Somewhat Very	1 2 3 4 5 6 7 8 9 10 — Unable Some Skill Proficient
Analysis	1 2 3 4 5 6 7 8 9 10 — None Somewhat Very	1 2 3 4 5 6 7 8 9 10 — Unable Some Skill Proficient
Synthesis	1 2 3 4 5 6 7 8 9 10 — None Somewhat Very	1 2 3 4 5 6 7 8 9 10 — Unable Some Skill Proficient
Clarification	1 2 3 4 5 6 7 8 9 10 — None Somewhat Very	1 2 3 4 5 6 7 8 9 10 — Unable Some Skill Proficient

To complete the gap analysis, find the skill that was most important to the success of the team, but also the one that the team was least able to perform (the skill that has the highest ranking and lowest rating).

FILL IN SKILL

This skill represents the biggest gap in competency for the team. Some of the ways that the team might address this gap in competency are:

1. identify someone in the team who would like to develop this competency and provide assistance or training;
2. recruit a new member to the team who has this competency;
3. have the team determine a way that the entire team can learn this skill.

The gap analysis is a good way to help the team establish its priorities for learning.

Team Work

Considering what you have learned about the skills of past teams and the value of the gap analysis, apply this learning to a current team.

What are the most important skills for your team to have, given the task they have been charged to complete?

_____ _____ _____

What are the skills your team performs least well?

_____ _____ _____

What are the most important skills for your team to develop?

_____ _____ _____

How could you best learn/acquire these skills? _____

_____

Team Charter

Record your ideas, suggestions, and decisions in the Team Charter in the appendix of the book.

Not every team member must have the same complement of skills. While there is a general level of skill in each area that all team members must have, the team can also draw on specific expertise from members within and outside the team. The team must decide which skills are broad and important enough for it to acquire for both team and personal development, and which skills the team simply needs to access.

Organizations have often wasted time and money giving employees extensive team training before assigning them to teams. Since broad training is, necessarily, out of context with what each person's team may need, the learning is usually minimal. If an organization wishes to do initial team training, it would be better to provide general information on the purpose and expectations of teams within the overall organization structure and focus primarily in the area of teaching team members how to identify and develop the skills the team will need to accomplish its goals. As the team develops, it can then decide what additional training it requires. Identifying areas for mutual learning is a good way for the team to develop both task and relationship skills.

STABILITY

Much of the early research done on teams stressed the need for stability in team membership in order to build cohesive teams. This recommendation is at odds both with the dynamics in today's organizations and the need for teams to be very fluid. Organizations need teams that can respond to a changing environment with changing members and changing goals. Teams, therefore, need to be structured in a way that allows for the benefits of stability and the vitality of change.

Given the degree and speed of change in the organization today, it is important that teams be robust and able to gel quickly. Robustness speaks to the ability of the team to endure, given changes in membership, task, and environment. Just as with a "robust" product, teams need to be able to be "dropped" several times and still work. Each of the four dimensions of team effectiveness discussed in this book (structure, process, culture, and politics) adds to the robustness of the team. For the structural dimension of a team, robustness comes in design.

The structural goal is to design a team that is both stable and fluid. To address this paradox it is helpful to look to a model for structuring flexible organizations presented by C. Handy in *The Age of Unreason*. To increase the organization's ability to respond to change, Handy suggests a shamrock structure that has three types of employees. This structure would also work well with teams.

The shamrock team structure includes three kinds of members: core, expert, and support. The core members of the team, as few as four and as many as ten, have the key responsibility for achieving the team purpose. These core team members will tend to stay together for the life of the team and will need to spend a great deal of time together to develop the purpose, process, and culture of a strong team.

Expert members, rather than being permanent to the team, come and go as the team's work progresses. However, expert members are not just visitors to the team. They may have a long-term commitment to the team but just not need to have a continuous presence. An example of an expert member of a team might be the engineer with special technical expertise who will contribute throughout the development of a project but with different intensity at different times. Another example might be the involvement of a customer on a product development team. The customer has a long-term and serious role on the team but does not necessarily need to have continuous involvement. In the culture section (Chapter 8), we will discuss how to smoothly bring these members in and out of the team to ensure their effectiveness.

Support members of the team are called upon for special projects. Examples might be co-workers needed to put on a major trade show or external workers hired to address a seasonal spike in business. To achieve maximum effectiveness in their role on

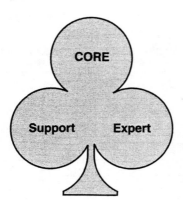

Fluid Team Structure

the team, the core members of the team must develop mechanisms for support members to be focused, managed, and valued.

A shamrock structure allows teams to maintain a manageable small size but still have wide use of expertise and personnel when needed. The shamrock structure also allows for people to come and go, adding to the perspective of the team and thereby decreasing the chance that the team will become isolated.

Reflection

Reflecting on your role as a member of a team, how well was the team able to deal with the dynamics of change?

To what extent was the team able to withstand and capitalize on changes in membership?

_____
_____
_____

To what extent was the team able to shift its focus when necessary without resenting a change in direction?

_____
_____
_____

To what extent was the team able to draw in and value the external expertise and support resources it needed?

_____
_____

What specific things did the team do that made change easier to embrace?

_____
_____

Team Work

Translate your past experiences to your current team.

How could you increase the flexibility of your team? _____
_____
_____

Who might be included as "experts" on your team? _____
_____
_____

How could you take advantage of expert and support members for the team?

_____
_____
_____

How would you make them an effective part of the team? _____
_____
_____
_____

Team Charter

Record your ideas, suggestions, and decisions in the Team Charter in the appendix of the book.

From this chapter you can see that there are several key decisions that organizations and teams must make to give teams the best chance for success. Membership in the team must provide the skills, information, and commitment necessary to complete the team's charge. The team needs to formally and regularly assess what it needs to learn. Learning can take place with knowledge and skill acquisition by the team or by bringing in team members with needed expertise. Whatever the choice, capability is the goal. Finally, traditional expectations of stability within the team are probably unrealistic in today's organization. Change within and outside the team is now the norm, and effective teams find ways to be flexible without losing cohesion. The topics in this chapter are items to address before the team becomes focused on its task. Often these items are taken for granted. Successful organizations make them part of the original team design.

CHAPTER 2

Clarifying Purpose

Learning from this chapter:

■ To understand the value and process of team purposing activities.

■ To explain the need for and ability to develop goals for team success.

■ To understand the value of team measures and be able to design task and process measures.

Other things I want to learn about defining team purpose:

■

■

Purpose

intencja
pnzeznachenie
cel
zamiar
zamysl
miec na celu

Perhaps the single most important activity a team engages in is clearly defining its purpose. The process of purposing requires that the team answer the following questions:

• Why are we here?
• What do we want to accomplish?
• How will we know if we are successful?

Most teams do not spend enough time on this activity and pay great future penalties as the team struggles with accountability and acceptance of their ideas and recommendations.

The first question, Why are we here?, requires the team to clarify the reason why it was formed in the first place. Earlier we discussed how common it is for organizations to form teams with only the most general rationale. The team, therefore, often finds itself in the position of having to clarify its existence. To do this, team members need to discuss their perceptions of why they think the team has been formed and why they, in particular, have been asked to serve on the team.

This purposing exercise needs to clarify two things: First, the degree of understanding among team members about their purpose, and second, each person's interest in being on the team. It is not necessary that each person have the same understanding of purpose or the same interest and commitment to membership. It *is* necessary that the differences in team member perceptions be expressed and understood so that they do not bring serious conflicts to the team.

An example will serve to illustrate this point. A large organization decided that it needed to address the issue of diversity within its organization. The concept of diversity and its potential for being either a great asset or a great liability had become a topic of interest and discussion within the organization. Top management decided that it needed a "diversity council" to advise them on this issue and to assure itself that the increasing diversity in the organization stayed on the asset side. Management selected members from the organization to serve on the council and called them together.

The team had 22 members. There were representatives from different ethnic and racial groups as well as physically challenged persons and other people who represented the different job levels in the organization (professional, technical, and support). Thus the team was heterogeneous in terms of both level in the organization and personal attributes. In addition, two team coaches from management were assigned to the team. The directive to the team was to advise management on diversity issues.

The team met several times but was having great trouble settling on a plan for action. Worse, with each meeting there were increasingly hostile feelings among team members. Since the team had not clarified its purpose, individual members tried to force the team to address her or his current issue at team meetings. Tug-of-wars for attention became the norm, and no issue was worked to conclusion. This inability to reach agreement was probably just as well, for there would have been no true support for any team action. Management became aware of the team's struggles and called in a facilitator to help the team get realigned.

The main problem was that the team had never done any "purposing." Team members were unclear about why the team existed and about the kind of issues they should address. Some members of the group wanted to deal with current employee grievances. They wanted the council to be a "hearing board" for employees to present their diversity problems. Others argued that Human Resources already played that role and that the council should not deal with personal or personnel issues. Those members advocated playing a policy role, though they were unclear what kind of policy they should address.

Without a common purpose, each representative was focused on his/her own agenda; that is, people on the team, because of racial/ethnic background, wanted to address those issues; the physically challenged people wanted to discuss barriers within the organization; and the job class representatives were generally unclear about how they fit into the diversity issue at all.

Without a clear purpose, teams begin to focus on problems and differences.

These differences degenerated into arguments. Each meeting became more polarized. At the inception of the team, the two coaches from management decided not to be team leaders but only to become involved when requested to do so by the team. Thus, there was no appointed leadership for the team and no mechanism for drawing leadership from within the team. The diversity council was clearly in danger of becoming a fiasco, resulting in the one thing all the members did not want to do—show diversity as a liability rather than an asset to the organization.

With a facilitator the team was able to clarify its purpose. Together the group defined several roles they could play in the organization, from being a member of the hearings council to problem solver to policy advisor. Then team members asked for a meeting with the management group that had organized them. They discussed their options with management to clarify the original intent for the team. The result of the discussion moved the team's purpose toward the policy end of the responsibility choices.

Management did not want the council to be a grievance board. They wanted the council to look at ways to help members of the organization to understand diversity issues and to enable the organization to draw on diversity as an asset. If the council came upon general problems/barriers to diversity in the organization, management wanted to know about them, but the group was not to be an internal audit unit.

Teams need to purpose frequently.

Armed with its new information, the diversity council began to gel. They formed subgroups to develop ideas for the council to consider. Some of the subgroups were focused on a single issue; others took a more general approach to diversity. Some of the ideas the council eventually brought to fruition included: a calendar that identified all the different holidays represented by the different ethnic groups in the organization; monthly examples in the newsletter of diversity at work in the organization, with a particular emphasis on nontraditional aspects of diversity, such as different approaches to thinking; automatic entry doors to assist the physically challenged; and ethnic specialties in the cafeteria to coincide with a specific ethnic awareness event or holiday. The council learned to work together and to value each other's issues. They were able to reach the goal of increasing awareness of diversity within the organization and demonstrate how diversity increased the effectiveness of the organization.

The learning from this example is that once the team defined its purpose, it was able to capitalize on member differences and use them to the team's advantage. It was also able to identify goals and make progress. Without a clear purpose, teams begin to focus negatively on internal problems and differences. Team members find and call attention to the shortcomings of individual team members and take sides on issues. With a clear and compelling purpose, the team can accommodate individual peculiarities and ignore annoyances for the sake of accomplishment.

Reflection

Consider when you have been a member of a team that has been charged with a complex and/or ambiguous task.

What useful things did the team do to clarify its purpose? _____
_____
_____

What dysfunctional things did the team do that confused the issue or forced people to harden their positions? _____
_____
_____

What can you learn about establishing team purpose from reflecting on this team's successes and failures? _____
_____
_____

Team Work

Translate this learning to a current team.

What do you think is your team's purpose? _____
_____

To what extent do you think the other members of the team would agree with you?
_____ How might their views of purpose differ from yours?
_____

What areas of purpose need to be continually clarified? _____

What should the team do to assure that the team purpose is, and remains, clear and supported? _____

Team Charter

Record your suggestions, ideas, and decisions in the Team Charter in the appendix of the book.

Defining a clear purpose is not a panacea for all team issues, and purposing is not a one-time event. Even with a clear purpose, the team needs to deal with process problems. The purpose simply puts those process issues in context and allows the team to work on them in a more constructive manner. For example, people on the diversity council would, on occasion, take an employee complaint to the meeting table and urge the council to take it on. The team would use purpose to keep itself on track and refer the complaint to Human Resources. Purpose allowed the team to redirect the concerned team member's issue without personalizing the person's inappropriate behavior. In addition, the discussion reinforced and clarified the team's reason for being and developed useful feedback skills among team members.

Teams need to purpose frequently. The more complex or controversial their charge and/or team composition, the more they need to purpose. In its beginning stages, the team may need to validate/clarify its purpose every time it meets. In times of great change the team must purpose to understand the impact of any internal or external change on its purpose. Circumstances may render the team unnecessary or ineffective, or change the urgency of its task from moderate to extreme. If so, the team needs to address the change so it does not waste time meeting around the wrong purpose.

Purposing takes time. To be effective, the team must be willing to spend the time and energy necessary to clarify purpose. Teams that rush to action or fill agendas with tasks and save no room for discussing the larger team focus of those tasks will repeatedly find themselves off course.

Purposing requires a certain amount of nondirected discussion. Members need to get to know each other's values and perspectives on the team's task. These are best brought out in an open and general discussion, rather than through an agenda item that seeks to "list" team member perspectives. We will discuss a conversation technique called dialog later as a method for effective decision making. However, dialog can be very useful for team purposing as well.

An important part of purposing is defining the commitment of each team member to the purpose of the team. People come to the team with very different expectations of contribution and payback. It is not necessary that everyone on the team have the same commitment/contribution level. It is important that the team understand those different levels and design team activities in accordance. For example, referring to the shamrock structure discussed in the previous chapter, if a person sees his/her contribution to the team to be quite narrow in scope, perhaps that person should be an "expert" member of the team, rather than a "core" member. The team then needs to define the role and expectations of being an expert member rather than a core member and be sure there is agreement on the defined role.

The key to building an effective team is to be willing to customize the roles people will play. Too often we have only one model for team commitment. Everyone is expected to be committed to the same things, in the same way, and at the same level. That

An important part of purposing is defining the commitment of each team member to the purpose of the team.

Teams need to purpose frequently. The more complex or controversial their charge and/or team composition, the more they need to purpose.

is simply an unrealistic and unnecessary burden. The team needs to find out what each member is willing to contribute and what is expected as payback. Then, from a team purpose perspective, members can decide if they need more or different membership and how the current membership should come together to achieve results. Later we will discuss commitment again as an element of team culture, with suggestions for understanding and building the commitment level among team members.

Whatever the specific contribution, team members must accept and understand that they have a mutual accountability for team accomplishment. The team succeeds or fails as a team. Goal definition, task assignments, process rules and evaluation, culture creation, and external interactions must all be defined with mutual accountability in mind. Each team member has a role to play, but these roles come together to achieve a common result.

Addressing purpose and goals is often not easy for a team. In a culture like that in the US, where action, any action, is preferable to inaction, teams struggle with taking the time to focus. Since purposing is a cerebral activity that requires sharing values and sometimes feelings, the process can be uncomfortable. Skills that draw out understanding and clarify interests are often not well developed, so purposing and goal setting can be reduced to nit picking arguments where people are willing to walk out over the use of a given word or inclusion of a given goal. Though it is usually obvious to a team that they need a clear purpose, it is not uncommon to have the team rush through the process. Unfortunately, the more the team needs to establish a clear purpose, the more difficult it often becomes.

To illustrate the point, let's look at a team that struggled mightily over purpose. The team was the senior management of a large health care organization. The twelve members of the team represented the major operating divisions of the unit including the hospital, urgent care, and long-term care. Also represented were functional areas including quality assurance, finance, human resources, administration, and MIS. As with any health care entity in today's business environment, they were besieged with problems. Costs were rising rapidly, standard of care was a battleground, and competition was very tough. In fact, the organization was in very serious danger of failing.

The head of the organization called the team together to determine a plan for action. The team met several times but was never able to identify a course of action that all could commit to. They identified key problems but argued over specific data. They identified competitive threats but could not decide what to do about them. No one was willing to give up anything for the common good; each was first of all concerned with maintaining his or her own position.

This example is useful because it illustrates the illusive nature of purpose. This team knew they were called together to save the organization, but they did not clarify what that meant. They engaged in a great deal of activity, especially analysis, speculation, and blame. It was not that they did not put in the time. They met for many, many hours, but they engaged in superficial, nonfocused discussion. Eventually, they ran out of time and the organization was sold.

The lesson learned is that purpose must be clear and bold and demand real work from team members. It must also have elements that every member can buy into. You cannot order a team to achieve purpose; they have to want to achieve it. Goals must be specific and people must be committed and held responsible. The conversation must be both passionate and focused.

One of the ways to get a team to discuss purpose and commit is to draw out the assumptions team members hold about the team or the task. Once team members bring their different assumptions out on the table they can challenge them, create new expectations, or decide to accept the current assumption. Using the health care management team as an example, some assumptions likely to be found in the team would include:

1. We need to keep the organization structure the same.
2. The hospital is the source of all of our problems.
3. We just need to cut costs, but I've done all I can.

Once these assumptions are on the table the team can address them. For example, it would not take long for the team to realize that they would not get far with cost cutting if everyone looked to the other person for sacrifice. Since the hospital was a critical part of the health care organization, the entire team needed to accept responsibility for resolving the issues that the hospital faced. The team could then move from blaming to problem solving.

Reflection

Think about a time when you have been on a team and consider the assumptions you brought to the team.

Some of your assumptions:

1. _____

2. _____

3. _____

In retrospect, do you think that they were valid? _____
_____

How do you think the assumptions of the other team members would be different from yours?
_____
_____
_____

How do you think those different assumptions impacted team performance?
_____
_____
_____

Team Work

Translate this learning to a current team.

What are your assumptions about this team's task? _____

_____

What are your assumptions about this team's process?_____

_____

How could you validate your assumptions against those of the other members of the team?
_____
_____
_____

How might you go about getting the team to challenge these assumptions?
_____
_____
_____

Team Charter

Record your suggestions, ideas, and decisions in the Team Charter in the appendix of the book.

Goals

CEL

Once the team has defined its purpose, it needs to establish goals. Goals provide the team with the specific outcomes that drive both the organization of, and the motivation for, effort. Without goals the team will simply drift from activity to activity and never feel a sense of accomplishment.

Let's consider an example that is common when the market changes and there is a need to change strategy to remain competitive. A manufacturing company found itself in serious financial trouble. The head of the company brought the managers of the various business units (product managers, regional managers, and plant managers) and department heads (MIS, Human Resources, Finance, Manufacturing, Engineering, etc.) together as a team to address the problem. While most of the members of the group had met together in various configurations, this was the first time that this particular combination of people had met.

As a group, they identified that they needed to expand the business into international markets because the domestic market would not provide for company growth. In fact, they spent weeks defining the areas where they wanted to do business. However, they were unable to establish clear goals that they could agree to. As a group, they were so concerned about making a mistake that they were reluctant to start in any direction. Individually, they were so intent on preserving the organizational structure and the position and resources of their own entities that they could not define a different future for the organization. The only goals they could agree to were activity-based goals, such as gathering more information about competitors, defining the internal problems, and presenting analysis. When someone would suggest a goal, the members of the group would challenge it or offer counter proposals, with the result that no one could ever agree on one, or for that matter, parallel courses of action. Unfortunately, this example did not result in a positive resolution. The group continued to founder and the financial situation got worse. The company was purchased by others, the entity broken up, and individual parts sold off.

The lesson learned here is that the problem was not caused by the group taking the wrong action, but by taking no action. The group literally talked themselves out of existence. Teams have a tendency to search for the one goal or path. This often leads to analysis paralysis and an unwillingness to move for fear that the move might not be the "right" one. It is important for teams to set initial goals and to begin a course of action.

There are two methods that can ease the team's concern about making a mistake. The first is to set initial short-term goals so that the team can "test the water" as it moves down a given path. Another method, often more useful, is to follow multiple paths at once. In the case of our manufacturing management team, they got so caught up in looking for the major right course of action that they failed to pursue the multiple resolutions available to them.

Research and experience show that milestones should have a horizon of not more than 90 days. Most people cannot manage the ambiguity of time beyond that. Events that are a year away seem unmanageable. New teams or teams dealing with highly complex or controversial tasks may need monthly milestones. For these teams it is important that members identify, early on, any need for course correction. If the team gets off on the wrong path, it may be difficult for it to recover.

Milestones are usually associated with task assignments, but the team also needs to set process goals and milestones. Team members often neglect these goals, thinking they will naturally evolve into an effective team. However, effective team behaviors do not just simply evolve. They need to be consciously developed. In the last chapter, we talked about the need for the team to learn new skills. Setting process goals can provide an opportunity for the team to identify and advance in its learning. Process goals help the team define how it wants to work together and how each member wants to grow as a result of his or her team experience.

Process goals a team might strive for include:

- efficiency of decision-making process
- creativity in generating options
- trust in fellow team members and those outside the team
- quality of analytical process
- usefulness of data presentation
- quality and equity of participation

Reflection

Identify a team that you have been part of for at least six months. Using the quarterly calendars below, record the accomplishments of the team. Include both process and task successes.

Team Accomplishments				
Quarter 1	*Week 1*	*Week 2*	*Week 3*	*Week 4*
First Month				
Second Month				
Third Month				
Quarter 2	*Week 1*	*Week 2*	*Week 3*	*Week 4*
First Month				
Second Month				
Third Month				

Are you satisfied with the team accomplishments? _____

Was the team able to accomplish both process and task goals? _____
_____

How do you think your other team members' assessments would differ from yours?
_____

Team Work

Now use the calendars in a future fashion. For your current team, indicate the achievements the team has identified for the next six months. Be sure to include both process and task targets.

Future Achievements				
Quarter 1	*Week 1*	*Week 2*	*Week 3*	*Week 4*
First Month				
Second Month				
Third Month				
Quarter 2	*Week 1*	*Week 2*	*Week 3*	*Week 4*
First Month				
Second Month				
Third Month				

What special efforts will it take to meet these goals? _____

_____

Team Charter

Record your suggestions, ideas, and decisions in the Team Charter in the appendix of the book.

Coming together for the sake of being a team and even enjoying time together is not enough to allow a team to prosper and endure. Activity-driven teams that focus on meeting rather achieving will drive out achievement-oriented team members. The team needs to feel that it has an important purpose, that it will make a contribution to the organization or unit. Goals, therefore, become the manifestation of the team's purpose, and results become the tangible product of the team's work.

Measures

Goals without measures are fantasies. It is relatively easy to make a goal; measures give real meaning to those goals. Teams need to establish measures for each area of responsibility. Therefore, general team measures need to reflect:

- Indicators of continued appropriateness of the goal
- Progress toward content goals
- Progress toward process goals
- Evidence of individual team member growth and development

Team measures suffer from all the problems of other measures we use in the organization. Chief among these problems is that we often fear the information coming from the measure. That is, we fear failure. It is important to realize, however, that you may avoid the evidence of failure if you avoid measurement, but you will also miss success. For, without measures, there is also no evidence of achievement.

One way to encourage teams to measure is to focus on collecting positive information. We have a tendency to collect information on what went wrong rather than on what went well, and as a result, measurement information often brings bad news. If possible, we can change the measure to a positive indicator, such as:

Goals without measures are fantasies.

- How many people outside the team were included in the discussion of a sensitive issue?
- How often did the team achieve a milestone and what helped the team succeed?
- Who supports our proposal and how can we capitalize on that support?
- What have we learned to do that we could not do before?
- What partnerships have we developed and how can we best use them?
- What information have we gathered and how can it help us?

There is an old adage that offers wise advice for measurement.

If you know what you are doing wrong,
you must still figure out what to do right;
If you know what you are doing right, all
you have to do is do it over and over again.

We must, and will always need to, measure our problems and difficulties. But a balance in measuring successes and errors will take us a long way toward helping teams embrace measurement as a valuable tool and accept the information that measures can provide.

Teams continually need to validate the appropriateness of their goals. This means that on a regular basis the team needs to check with its constituencies to determine whether it should continue its work and proceed in the current direction. Those constituencies might include the management team that initiated the team, the people who will implement the ideas of the team, and the team members themselves.

Examples of ways a team might measure goal relevance include:

- Re-examine the language of the original goal of the team to see that it still reflects important work.
- Ask the group who initiated the team to define how they would recognize progress and success toward the purpose.
- Hold feedback sessions with those who will implement the work of the team to see if they are still supportive of the team's work.
- Compare accomplishments with other teams in the overall product/service process to assure that the team's success has not hampered the efforts of others.

The information on external focus given later will give you further ideas on how to measure the effectiveness of the work of the team in terms of meeting external expectations.

Measuring progress towards the team's goal needs to be a regular part of the team's activity. The key to developing useful measures is to measure frequently and to use multiple indicators of progress. If the team has short-term measures, it can identify problems before they become true obstacles. The longer the team waits to measure, the more likely one or more team members will have a vested interest in pursuing the current path of the team. Those members will be reluctant to explore data that suggest a change in direction.

Frequent measures also help the team feel a sense of accomplishment. An example of one such measure is the thermometer scales used by many fundraising groups. As their fundraising progresses, the "mercury" on the thermometer continues to rise. People see the progress and want to be part of the successful effort.

Measures must provide the team with information as well as judgment. To simply say the team hit or missed its target is often not very helpful. It needs to know what went well so that it can do it again and improve on it. The team also needs to know what went poorly so it can change. If the team only knows hit or miss, performance becomes a mystery, a random event over which the team has little control. The team will quickly tire of gambling and find other more predictable ways to spend its time. The value of using multiple indicators rather than just one measure is that various indicators serve as diagnostics pinpointing the source of the deficiency. Examples of multiple indicators for a team process goal of improved decision making might be:

- Decision making is less time consuming
- Decisions are not revisited unless important new information has surfaced
- More information is being brought into the decision-making process; decisions are more data driven
- More team members are actively involved in decision-making discussion
- At least three alternatives are generated and explored for each key decision
- At least one outside person is brought in to represent a new perspective

The more the team can view measures as a natural and useful part of purposing, the less resistance the team will have to measurement information. Measures need to be established when goals are set. If the team waits until performance becomes an issue, the team is likely to deny or manipulate the measure. If used as justification rather than information, measures can drive a team into cover up. Self-assessment and course correction are indicators of the maturity and commitment of the team.

Reflection

Refer to the achievement calendar in the previous section.

What indicators did the team use to show progress toward task goals? _____
_____

What indicators did the team use to show progress on process goals? _____
_____

Which of the indicators used by the team were negative measures? _____
_____

What recommendations would you make to improve the measurements the team used? _____
_____

Team Work

Refer to the future achievement calendar in the previous section. Choose key goals and identify and indicator of success and concern for each.

Possible Measures		
Key Goal	*Indicator for Success*	*Indicator for Concern*

How might you get your team to commit to these measures? _____

_____

_____

How might you collect information for these measures? _____

_____

_____

Team Charter

Record your suggestions, ideas, and decisions in the Team Charter in the appendix of the book.

As important as measures are, they are not ends unto themselves. They must lead to action, not consume all the team's energy just doing the measure. A story that describes the kinds of measures that are helpful to a team follows.

> There was a very successful CEO of a lumber mill who was about to retire. Shortly before leaving his successor came to him for advice. What was it, the new CEO wanted to know, that had made his predecessor so successful. The retiring CEO went to his window that overlooked the mill and pointed to the smokestacks. "I keep a close eye on the smoke" he said. "If the smoke is white everything is going well and I can go about my business. If the smoke turns gray there is trouble brewing and I need to gather information on what is going on. If the smoke turns black I go directly to the mill and find out the source of the problem."

The moral of the story is that it is important for the team to keep a constant eye on major indicators of team progress. Those indicators need to include both task and process measures. For example, indicators for task might be:

- Reaching short-term objectives
- Regularly meeting deadlines
- Satisfaction with quality of work within and outside the team
- Continued support by sponsoring person or unit

Like the wise manager, the team must identify key indicators and then watch them carefully. When the "smoke" turns to gray it is time to invest in more specific indicators so the smoke does not turn black.

Developing key measures of team process is also important to ensuring the effectiveness of the team. As we have stated, teams do not develop without effort. The team must pay attention to how it is operating and measure the extent to which it is meeting its expectations. Some of the key process measures that need to be taken on a regular basis include:

- Level of trust among team members
- Evidence of open communication and constructive conflict
- Evidence of creative thinking and innovative ideas
- Commitment and equivalent participation among members
- Level of energy and enthusiasm for team tasks
- Decision-making efficiency and support for decisions made

These process issues will be discussed in detail as you go through the other chapters of the book. In addition, in the appendix there is a periodic review which offers measures that can be used regularly to monitor the effectiveness of the team process and task achievement.

For team members to maintain interest in the team, they must feel that they are getting some personal benefit from membership. This is especially true in cultures like that in the United States which value individualism and personal achievement. For a team to be effective, both members and team must learn, improve, and reach goals.

Each person on the team needs to set personal goals for growth through the team experience. Just as the team needs to take progress checks, so does the individual. Some of the indicators that a team member is benefiting from the team experience include:

- Acquired new technical information
- Able to play a more effective role in group decision making
- Improved interpersonal skills
- Exposure to constituencies that would not have been available outside the team
- Increased self-esteem
- Better sense of the overall direction and functioning of the organization

In summary, purposing is at the heart of effective teams. Nothing can match the staying power of an important cause. Without a keen sense of purpose the team cannot weather the turbulence of team life. Purpose holds the team together and gives a reason for resolving team problems.

Teams are able to maintain their focus on purpose through goals and measures. Without evidence of progress and success, purpose is only an illusion. Successful teams set short- and long-term goals and identify key measures that will help them understand how to continue and improve their performance.

Given the expense and effort required to bring teams together, it is essential that organizations encourage, perhaps even require, that teams learn purposing skills and take the time necessary to do purposing well.

Leadership

Learning from this chapter:

- To understand the effects of external leadership on the success of the team.

- To be able to describe the role of coach in the team process.

- To be able to compare and contrast the internal leadership choices available to a team.

- To be able to assess the level of positive leadership within a team.

Other things I want to learn about teams and leadership:

-
-

In the area of organizational management, the concept of leadership has intrigued scholars and practitioners alike. Years of work have gone into understanding the concept of leadership, prescribing leader behaviors and developing leadership skills. As the use of teams increases in the organization, this concern over leadership is extending to teams. If teams are to be a major work unit in the organization, ways to direct both team members and the team process must be developed.

When discussing team leadership, our focus comes from two perspectives: leadership provided from outside the team and leadership developed within the team. Appropriate expressions of both forms of leadership must be present for the team to function well.

Leadership Provided from Outside the Team

Management must provide direction for the team without interfering with the team's ownership of purpose and process. As we look at the evolution of organizational teams, especially since the mid-1970s, with the emphasis productivity improvement initiatives placed on teamwork and the creation of quality circles, the role of the manager with regard to the team has been a perplexity. Until the productivity improvement movement, teams were not recognized as a fundamental working unit of the organization. People were gathered into functional groups that operated in hierarchical fashion with the individual members taking direction from the manager and leader of the unit. Position power was the basis for group leadership. That is, the senior person directed the individual work of each person in the functional group. Leadership was synonymous with direction, and a functional group was the closest approximation an organization had to a team.

As quality circles emerged, especially with the performance success of the Quality of Work Life teams at the Volvo Plant in Sweden, organizations began to consider that functional groups were different from teams and that teams could do some work by themselves. The Quality circle was the first team model that could be called self-led.

A self-led team is one where the team accepts the primary responsibility for directing team efforts and achieving team results. Self-led teams are quite different from the earlier model of manager-led teams where the success or failure of the team was seen as the responsibility of the manager. It is easy to see that if the manager was held accountable for team results, then he or she was going to exert as much control as possible over team process. Thus, control is often seen as being at the heart of the team leadership issue.

Self-led teams have some very attractive attributes, including decision making by the workers who have the best information about the work, and the development of team members into broader-thinking, cross-trained human resources. But the nagging problem of control remains. What is the role of the manager in this new model of self-led team?

If the manager is completely left out of the team, there is great fear that anarchy will reign in the organization. The author's experience is that when a manager has minimal interaction with the team, anarchy is, indeed, a very real possibility and not just a paranoid fear. Without guidance, a team often takes on issues that are inappropriate for its membership and often begins to think of itself as an isolated source of action without responsibility or accountability to the larger organization.

For example, when organizations began to use quality circles to address problems within the organization, they often took on a life of their own. In the spirit of involvement, the teams were, in fact, often encouraged by management to "find a problem and solve it." The result was that teams often responded in inappropriate or unappreciated ways. Some teams identified problems the organization was not interested in addressing. Other teams offered solutions that were inappropriate: requiring an inappropriate financial investment by the organization, interfering with the workings of other units, or placing the issue at a level of urgency and importance that was not warranted.

Management found itself in a very uncomfortable position. If it accepted the inappropriate recommendations of the teams, it would be expending unnecessary effort or spending money unwisely. In addition, it was not improving the team's problem-solving skills or value to the organization to implement ill-conceived decisions. Worst of all, management was in danger of losing strategic control of the organization.

If it rejected the suggestions of the team, anger and frustration prevailed, and the level of cynicism within the organization increased. Team members attacked both the wisdom and integrity of management and often the problem situation became worse than it was before the team addressed it. Managers began to wonder if teams were really worth the effort, and interest in quality circles waned toward the mid-1980s.

The Total Quality Management effort of the late '80s and early '90s renewed organizations' interest in teams. Indeed, as management theory and knowledge has continued to evolve, it has become consistently apparent that teams are a critical component of an effective organization. It is becoming increasingly difficult for individuals to address, or even comprehend, the complex issues facing organizations today. Teams offer a way to bring needed information, perspective, and commitment to bear on an important organizational problem or opportunity. How to manage those teams, however, continues to be a dilemma.

As teamwork was combined with another Total Quality Management concept—empowerment—the issue of team control and leadership became more acute. Teams could be heard to declare themselves empowered and to tell management that the team needed to do whatever it thought best; any constraint or incursion by management was a violation of the virtue of empowerment. Empowerment was heady stuff for the organization to handle. In order for the organization to reap the benefits of speed and flexibility from TQM, it was apparent that teams needed to be given more power and control. But in a rush to gain influence and value in the organization, team members often ignored the accountability part of empowerment. The team was in charge; the team knew best. Full speed ahead!

As we look at the struggle for team leadership, it seems we are confusing order with control. Teams need to be tied to the strategic issues and direction of the organization if they are to make a significant contribution. This strategic tie provides order to the team. In most organizations, managers offer teams the best link to understanding those strategic initiatives, and therefore, are well suited to give a sense of order to the teams.

On the other hand, if management asserts a heavy hand of control on team process, it hampers team creativity and performance. Team members become reluctant to really take on their assignments. Challenging the manager/leader's preferred approach is considered politically dangerous if the manager is aggressive and/or vengeful. If the manager is more passive, team suggestions outside his or her preferred choice simply do not get implemented. Either way, teamwork is a waste of time.

One way that organizations have tried to address this need for control of the team is to take the external leadership away from the manager and vest it in a review board. In both productivity improvement and TQM initiatives, quality councils are set up to review and approve the recommendations of the teams. In theory this is sound, but in practice you do not sustain the interest and commitment of a team by rejecting its ideas. With an individual you may accept and reject recommendations with some regularity. But team work is much more complicated. By the time a team brings a recommendation to a management council, it has a vested interest in it. The team thinks the recommendation is the "right" one or it would not have invested such effort in developing it. To reject it is to reject the team, and to get the team to return to the table to rethink the issue is all but impossible. Our experience with teams is making it invariably clear that if teams are to contribute energy and initiative to solving organizational problems, the solutions they offer have to be accepted, either overtly through permission or covertly through empowerment. You cannot have teams spend effort and then reject the outcome.

So, what is management to do? How can the organization guide teams without controlling and limiting them? How can the organization enhance the viability of recommendations that come forward without hampering creativity? The resolution to this dilemma comes from having the leadership outside the team provide order rather than control. Leadership focused on order provides context for deliberation and discussion, advice for implementation, and skills for problems solving and decision making. The leadership role for managers in working with teams is one that favors guidance over control: the role of "coach" or "team sponsor." Managers do, indeed, have a role within the team, but it is a developmental and facilitative one, not a controlling one.

The role of coach or sponsor is very attractive in concept and does seem to be an appropriate way for managers to effectively work with teams in today's organizations. Only time will tell all that needs to be included in this role of coach, but at this point it appears that there are six key coaching behaviors that the manager needs to use with the team. These are:

Liaison.   As a liaison, the manager plays the coaching role of linking the team to other parts of the organization. Often teams would benefit from working with other units or even other organizations, but the team does not have the connections to facilitate this interaction. The coach can provide introductions and ease the sharing of information across groups. Rather than being a messenger or representative, an effective coach provides the team with the opportunity to develop its own relationships.

Resource provider.   Often a team does not have resources allocated to it as a specific entity. The manager's role as resource provider is to assist the team in defining its resource needs and then to secure those resources. The effective coach challenges the team to identify and justify its needs and then allocates or advocates for funds.

Counselor.   In this coaching role, the manager helps the team develop problem-solving skills. The coach helps the team adequately explore issues and consider alternatives. This is a process role for the coach, not an outcome role. That is, the effective coach does not judge or control the ideas of the team. Rather, she or he looks for ways to enhance the process of exploration and assessment of ideas taking place within the team.

Mentor.   As a mentor, the manager guides the team to develop organizational savvy. The coach helps the team understand the political realities of the issues and resolutions under consideration. Sharing his or her experience, the coach encourages the team to explore the broad context and implications for its decisions.

Teacher.   As a teacher, the manager provides or secures technical information for the team. This could include providing some uncommon or hard-to-acquire information, or securing data analysis training for team members. The effective coach uses the teacher role in an unbiased and trusting manner. The team needs to be allowed to assess and interpret the information it develops or acquires for itself.

Challenger.   At times the team needs someone to confront it. The manager in this coaching role must be willing to challenge the team on its decision-making process, its interpersonal relationships, and its progress toward task goals. This is sometimes a difficult role for the coach to play, but it is necessary if the team is to be self-reflective and to continuously improve. The effective coach is able to provide different and comparative insights into the team's effectiveness and efficiency. Comfort is not a sign that the team is working well. It may indicate that the team is unwilling or unable to improve. The coach must ensure that the team has an appropriate amount of constructive tension.

Reflection

Reflect on a team leader you have dealt with in the past and assess him or her on the chart below, using the coaching behaviors described above.

Team Leader Behaviors						
Controlling						*Coaching*
Represents team	1	2	3	4	5	Connects team
Controls resources	1	2	3	4	5	Provides resources
Makes decisions	1	2	3	4	5	Guides process
Withholds information	1	2	3	4	5	Shares information
Gives answers	1	2	3	4	5	Teaches skills
Scolds team, blames	1	2	3	4	5	Challenges to excel

How well did the leader's behaviors benefit the team? _____
_____

What could she or he have done better? _____
_____

Now, using a different color pen, assess your own team leader style. How well does your style match the need of teams in today's organizations?

_____

Team Work

With your current team, discuss your need for external leadership.

What coaching assistance does your team need? _____
_____
_____

How can you make the leadership you are receiving more effective? _____
_____
_____

Team Charter

Record your external leadership decisions, suggestions, and recommendations in the Team Charter in the appendix of the book.

One of the fundamental differences between the traditional role of team leader and the role of coach is the shift from telling to asking behaviors. Under the traditional model, managers were expected to have the right answers and to make the decisions. The manager's role was to share that knowledge with those who reported to him or her by telling them what to do.

In today's world, only the most arrogant or naive managers think they know all the answers. Rather than telling teams what to do, the effective coach guides the team through a series of helpful questions designed to draw out vital information on the issue at hand. With this information the team is able to move toward wise decisions, and the manager is then able to provide insight from experience without controlling the process.

Another very positive side effect to this coaching role of leadership is that everyone learns in the process. Team members learn what issues need to be considered in making decisions from a broader perspective, and the manager gains new insights into the values, priorities, and ideas of the people in the team.

Below are examples of the types of questions that managers might ask in each of the team coaching roles:

SOME QUESTIONS FOR THE COACH IN THE ROLE OF *LIAISON* TO ASK THE TEAM:
- Who has information that will help you understand this issue?
- How can I help you get this information?

SOME QUESTIONS FOR THE COACH IN THE ROLE OF *RESOURCE PROVIDER* TO ASK THE TEAM:
- What resources do you need to gather and analyze information?
- What resources do you need to be efficient decision makers?
- What resources do you need to develop and pursue an effective implementation process?

SOME QUESTIONS FOR THE COACH IN THE ROLE OF *COUNSELOR* TO ASK THE TEAM:

- Whose perspectives do you need to consider?
- What options have you developed? What are the advantages and disadvantages of each?
- What assumptions do you need to challenge?

SOME QUESTIONS FOR THE COACH IN THE ROLE OF *MENTOR* TO ASK THE TEAM:

- Who is likely to support this suggestion? Why? How can you capitalize on this support?
- Who is likely to resist this suggestion? Why? How can you neutralize that resistance?

SOME QUESTIONS FOR THE COACH IN THE ROLE OF *TEACHER* TO ASK THE TEAM:

- What do you need to learn to be able to address this issue?
- What level of expertise do you want to develop for this skill?
- What information do you need that you do not have easy access to?

SOME QUESTIONS FOR THE COACH IN THE ROLE OF *CHALLENGER* TO ASK THE TEAM:

- How will you deal with team members who do not meet their commitments?
- What must you do to meet your deadlines?
- How have you valued and taken into account the information you received from other units?

The coach role is extremely important for leadership in teams. Without involved managers, it is much more difficult for the team to be effective and for the manager to accept and develop the team. The manager needs to have a clear and important role with the team, but that role cannot be one of control. If the manager does not understand the coach role and does not learn the behaviors necessary to play the coaching role effectively, the team is weakened no matter how good the ideas it generates.

Leadership within the Team

Within teams, the key leadership issues that arise usually revolve around establishing roles and responsibilities for task accomplishment, fostering effective interaction among team members, and providing for team member development. As teams have evolved in organizations, terms such as self-managed and self-led teams have changed the concept of leadership within teams. Rather than leadership being provided through a manager as a designated chair, effective teams today define and carry out their own leadership roles. This change in internal leadership complements the change in external leadership for the team. As the team takes more ownership for its own leadership, the role of coach for the manager becomes more appropriate. The team needs guidance and support but can take care of directing its own actions.

Self-led teams are those whose members share the responsibility for accomplishing the team's purpose and take on planning, deciding, implementing, and evaluation responsibilities. For the self-led team, accountability and empowerment are complete. The team decides what it wants to do and does it. In addition, self-led team are responsible for managing both the internal culture and the external relationships of the team. Both of these issues will be discussed in detail in later chapters of the book. At this point it is enough to say that self-led teams are not only responsible for getting the job done but also for maturing the team and minding the needs of the organization. This is a very different kind of team than one whose success or failure is seen as the responsibility of the external leader or manager.

While self-management may be the ultimate desired end for a team, there are many steps along the way. In fact, the team can be quite effective without reaching the level of complete self-management, depending on its task and the relationship the team establishes with its coach and organization.

Figure 3.1 is a continuum of leadership for a team showing behaviors from being directed to being self-led.

At Level 1, the team follows the traditional model of receiving direction from a designated chair appointed by those outside the team. Team members follow the chair's lead and their contribution lies in fine-tuning the recommendations of the leader. Results are best gained through harmony and choosing noncontroversial actions through group agreement. These teams can have value in dealing with incremental changes where sharing information and cooperation are major goals of the team. Staff teams or task teams that have been called together to carry out a specific initiative often fall into this team category. An example might be when the organization takes on a campaign like raising funds for United Way. The team has little freedom around purpose, and its charge really is to cooperatively execute an order.

At Level 2, the team begins to exercise some influence over the team outcome. However, the success of the team is still vested in a person designated as chair. If the organization is wise and clear in its assignment of task, and the chair is willing and able to share with, and draw information from, the group, the team is able to contribute to the organization. Designing new ways of doing things within the current mindset is possible work for this team.

FIGURE 3.1 Continuum of Leadership

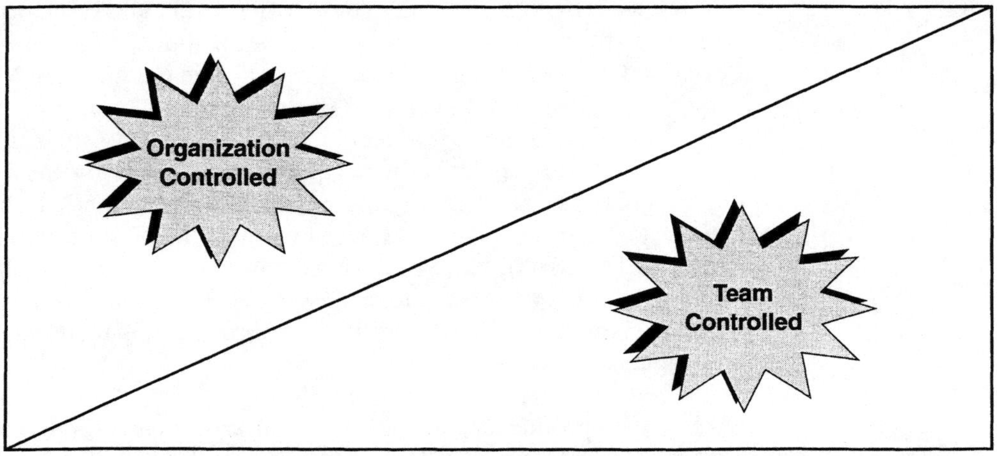

Level 1	Level 2	Level 3	Level 4
Goals and objectives given; chair designated; chair directs actions	Goals given; objectives developed; leadership from within; internal focus; static	Direction given; goals developed; shared leadership; coach used; team reaches out; grows	Team understands organizational strategy; has resources; shared leadership; external focus

An example of the work appropriate for this Level 2 team would be a situation in which a manager has received a complaint from a customer who has received the wrong merchandise. The manager calls together the people who took the order, filled the order, and shipped the order, and charges them with fixing the problem. The team starts to work on this narrow issue and is unlikely to consider forces outside its represented functions. This team is different from the team at Level 1 because it has more options to discuss and more flexibility to choose a course of action. Team members will take the solution to their manager for approval and will return to their own functional areas when a decision is made. Continuing the discussion/relationship after the specific problem is solved is unlikely. The team's work is done, and it has provided an opportunity for people to come together and solve the specific problem. The team structure and leadership at Level 2 do not encourage a more systemic look at addressing the issue.

There tends to be little development of individual member competencies in Level 2 teams since members primarily draw on their current skills, information, and perspectives. Teams at this level do not see themselves as dynamic; they focus on current issues and use conventional approaches in pursuing solutions.

At Level 3 the team is becoming a self-organizing unit and is taking on leadership roles. The team looks to the coach for advice and encouragement but defines its own path. At this point on the continuum the team begins to develop mutual accountability, realizing that whether the team fails or succeeds all members have a role to play.

Process improvement teams are often created with the expectation that they will operate at Level 3. Team members are given an overall assignment but are expected to set both goals and milestones for team progress. By design, most process improvement teams are cross-functional, so they need to understand different perspectives on issues and tend to pay attention to team process. To reach its goal of process improvement, the team always needs new information and usually needs new skills so the team has the opportunity to grow and develop. And, if the process improvement team is to be successful, it must draw in information from entities at both the input and output point of the process. Thus, the Level 3 team tends to be less isolated than teams further down the scale.

Teams at Level 3 are able to deal with conflict and think outside current mindsets with help from the coach. Since leadership responsibilities are shared and task skills developed at this level, individual members gain competency. Many organizations are very comfortable moving teams to this level.

At Level 4 the team is a nearly autonomous unit. Other than gaining general direction and resources from the organization, they are on their own. These teams require a great deal of maturity, and members develop many task and leadership skills. Process teams can evolve into Level 4 teams if the organization is willing to change its structure. The Saturn plant in Tennessee has been a leader in designing the organization around Level 4 process teams. Each process consists of a cross-trained team that sets its production schedule, secures resources, trains team members, and is held accountable as a team for results.

Where management is unwilling to totally structure their organizations around teams, a new product/service development process is a common candidate for a Level 4 team. Successful product/service development requires the support of many players in the organization. Since the process is naturally outcome focused around the new product or service, it is easier to assign resources and accountability to the team. The force that often keeps product/service development teams from developing into Level 4 teams is intervention by management. Instead of dealing with the team from a strategic viewpoint, top management often inserts a "pet project" into the process. This changes the leadership from within the group to outside the group and often pushes the team back down the leadership scale to a Level 2. This intervention robs the team of the creativity embedded in its multiple perspectives and destroys the sense of mutual accountability. If Level 4 teams are to work, leadership must operate as a strategic ally. Each side must make a distinct contribution, but neither side dominates nor directs. For organizations who want intrapreneurship, Level 4 teams are the level to strive for. Controlling the team is not an issue or concern for the organization; the team is working for itself.

As the team moves to self-management along the leadership continuum, there are various leadership roles that the team will develop. These leadership roles do not need to reside in one person. In fact, as the team moves toward self-management, they must belong to the team, not to the individual.

To understand this evolution from leadership vested in an individual to leadership vested in a team, we need a new vision of leadership. In the past, we have tried to break team leadership down into distinct skills and prescribe different roles for each person. This separation has robbed us of a holistic view of the nature of effective leadership and the culture that it creates.

Leadership, then, might be better viewed as a field of energy rather than as a summation of distinct roles. Adapting the application of "field" theory from quantum physics to leadership within self-led teams, as presented by Margaret Wheatley in *Leadership and the New Science,* leadership is an invisible force, like gravity, that affects everything the team does. It creates energy and waves of potential within the team. To paraphrase Meg Wheatley:

> We are bundles of potential moving through space. When we meet up with another energy source (a person), something is evoked from us—a behavior, reaction, or thought. New information and ideas are created when these energy sources meet.

This is an exciting description of a self-led team where leadership is a combined and spontaneous set of behaviors. Mutual accountability, as the hallmark of self-led teams, strives to assure that leadership exists within the team, not that the team has a leader. The team conscientiously measures its level of leadership to seek ways to grow.

If we accept the concept of leadership as a field, then we need to think about how to create that field within teams. To define leadership as a force that brings order and energy to the team is inspiring but not very helpful to teams who want this good sense of leadership. We need indicators to show when effective leadership exists and guidelines to help us learn and develop leadership behaviors.

James M. Kouzes and Barry Z. Posner, in *The Leadership Challenge* (San Francisco: Jossey-Bass, 1987), present a leadership model that can be adapted to define the concept of leadership within a team as a field of energy. They suggest that there are five different dimensions of leadership in the organization. If we use these dimensions as indicators, then we can determine the extent to which leadership exists within the team. From these guidelines we can describe behaviors that will enable teams to develop this type of leadership. What is unconventional here is that we want evidence that the TEAM exhibits these behaviors, not that they reside in a given individual.

Using the Kouzes and Posner dimensions, we must see that the following things occur in a team with:

- **A shared and inspired vision:**   Team members must be sure that they understand and believe in the team's purpose and that everyone in the team will grow from pursuing that vision. In the team this can be demonstrated by:
  1) The level of energy given the team task
  2) The quality of ideas coming from team
  3) The values displayed through team culture

- **Challenging team and task processes:** Team members must develop the skills and attitudes necessary to be innovative. In the team this can be demonstrated by:
  1) Use of constructive conflict in decision making
  2) Tolerance for diversity in people and responsibilities
  3) Ability to think outside current mindsets

- **Modeling team behavior:** Within the team, members must follow the ground rules they establish and commit the time and energy necessary for the team to define and achieve its purpose. In the team this can be demonstrated by:
  1) Use of effective facilitation skills
  2) Evidence of rituals supporting team rules and events
  3) Extent of sharing information with those inside and outside team

- **Enabling team members and others:** A characteristic of effective teams is that they strive to make each other successful and to build trust with those inside and outside the team. Everyone on the team must be better off for having been on the team. Relationships outside the team are based on partnerships. This can be demonstrated by:
  1) A high level of trust within the team and with external constituencies
  2) Evidence of continuous team learning and growth
  3) Development of self-esteem and confidence in team members

- **Encouraging the heart:** Teams are often given difficult tasks. Within the team there must be a supportive climate where individual talents and contributions are recognized and successes celebrated. In the team this can be demonstrated by:
  1) Public recognition of team member competency and expressed value of team members
  2) Rituals of celebration
  3) An ability to acknowledge and build on the ideas of others

Reflection

Reflect on a time when you were a member of a team with a complex and long-term task. Using the assessment tool on the next page, indicate the extent to which the team displayed effective behaviors.

Team Work

Now consider your current team using the same indicators. Which of these areas of leadership are strengths for the team? Which are areas for development?

Team Leadership Strength	*Team Leadership Development Need*

Which do you consider the most important area for attention? _____
_____

What can you do? _____
_____
_____

Team Charter

Record your suggestions, ideas, and decisions in the Team Charter in the appendix of the book.

Leadership is a critical aspect of effective team development. As we increase and expand our understanding of leadership, we see that it is more than just a role for one

Indicator	*Rating*				
Level of energy	1 Not evident	2	3 Sometimes displayed	4	5 Team competency
Quality of ideas	1 Not evident	2	3 Sometimes displayed	4	5 Team competency
Common values	1 Not evident	2	3 Sometimes displayed	4	5 Team competency
Constructive conflict	1 Not evident	2	3 Sometimes displayed	4	5 Team competency
Diversity	1 Not evident	2	3 Sometimes displayed	4	5 Team competency
Expanded mindsets	1 Not evident	2	3 Sometimes displayed	4	5 Team competency
Effective facilitation	1 Not evident	2	3 Sometimes displayed	4	5 Team competency
Ground rules reinforced	1 Not evident	2	3 Sometimes displayed	4	5 Team competency
Information sharing	1 Not evident	2	3 Sometimes displayed	4	5 Team competency
Level of trust	1 Not evident	2	3 Sometimes displayed	4	5 Team competency
Team learning/growth	1 Not evident	2	3 Sometimes displayed	4	5 Team competency
Self-esteem/confidence	1 Not evident	2	3 Sometimes displayed	4	5 Team competency
Members valued	1 Not evident	2	3 Sometimes displayed	4	5 Team competency
Achievements celebrated	1 Not evident	2	3 Sometimes displayed	4	5 Team competency
Acknowledge others	1 Not evident	2	3 Sometimes displayed	4	5 Team competency

person in the team to play. We are moving away from the concept that the team needs a leader, or even that the team needs several leaders, to a concept that suggests that teams need leadership. Leadership is an invisible force within a team that demonstrates itself in what and how the team addresses issues.

Developing leadership is one of the foundation pieces of the team puzzle, which is why it is included in the structure section of this book. In later chapters we will explore specific behaviors for decision making and problem solving which enhance the capability of leadership in the team and allow it to reach its goals.

Conclusion

Providing a sense of order and direction is critical to getting teams off to a good start. In this part of the book we have considered the elements that provide the foundation for team effectiveness. Specifically, we showed that care must be taken in the way that teams are brought into the organization. Management must clearly believe that the team initiatives they begin are consistent with the overall direction for the organization. In addition, individual teams must be wisely constituted with the right mix of participants and the appropriate amount of control.

Once the strategic intent of the use of teams is clear, the first work of the individual team is to define purpose and establish goals and measures. Without this the team has no reason for meeting and no method for sustaining energy and progress. On the process side of the team's effort, its first task is to determine how it will govern itself. Teams can operate on a continuum from being closely controlled to being self-led. The choice of level of control must reflect the maturity, skill, and purpose of the team. While most teams work toward self-management, it is not necessary to be a completely self-led team to add value to the organization.

As with any structure, the foundation determines the capability of the entire unit. Teams built with clear intent, solid membership, and an understanding of governance have the potential to bring great return to the organization. It is on this foundation that we will build the other sections of this book. In the next section we will discuss the characteristics of effective team process.

End of Section Activities

Discussion Questions

1. Describe the strategic impact of making teams a key part of the organization's structure.
2. Discuss the different types of teams available to the organization and the implications and situations for their use.
3. If you had the opportunity to build an ideal team, what would it look like?
4. Explain why defining purpose is such an important team task. What are the obstacles that teams often face when they begin to define purpose, and what are some ways to remove those obstacles?
5. Discuss the impact of external leadership on the success of the team. What leadership behaviors are useful when the team is externally managed?
6. Discuss the impact of internal leadership on the success of the team.
7. How can a team develop leadership without having *a* leader?

Application: Critical Incidents

1. You are the Director of a world-renowned museum. The museum has enjoyed many years of professional recognition and public interest. Funding for the arts is never easy, but the museum has done relatively well and has developed both grant writing and sponsor development skills.

You are just about to begin your strategic planning process. Traditionally, you plan on a five-year cycle, setting major long-term goals and then monitoring progress towards those goals. Every three years or so the Board of Directors comes together to validate the plan and make whatever adjustments are necessary. You are not so sure that this is the planning process to use this year. There are two major reasons for your misgivings.

First, the arts environment is in chaos because of cuts in funding and the impact of technology. Competition for funding is going to become much more competitive, and you are not sure your traditional methods will continue to be effective. Even more unnerving are the rapid changes in communication technology. Development of the Internet and the current capability of computers to use multi-media has changed the way people can experience the museum. These changes will impact not only what people expect when they visit the museum, but also the way they receive information about the alternatives they have to an actual visit.

The second change that impacts your planning process involves the culture the organization is fostering. Over the past few years the organization has become very participative, creating project teams and sharing decision making. Even the volunteer groups that support the museum have developed their own teams and have also become part of the organization teams. You are concerned that if the Board of Directors defines the direction of the organization and develops a plan as it has done in the past, it will not be embraced by the other stakeholders of the organization.

Given the concerns of the Director, how would you structure a strategic planning team for the organization?

2. You are the chief of a newly formed fire district. Over the past three years you have been involved in building facilities, securing equipment, and defining service levels. In addition, you have hired many fire fighters and have a traditional command and control staff in place.

Now that the basics are in place, you need to focus your attention on developing a management team. You expect that your organization will grow at a very rapid rate over the next five years, and that will mean the need for more facilities and more personnel. As the size of the department expands, it is becoming more difficult for you to manage all of the activities and issues that need attention.

You now have fifteen people on your management team, including fire captains and other program managers, administrative personnel, and an assistant chief. Most of these people have had very little experience in management, and while they are quite able, they need to begin to develop as a team.

What would you do, as Fire Chief, to start the team development process with this group of managers?

3. You are a department head in an organization that has been involved in Total Quality Management for about four years. Over the last year the organization has been re-engineering its various processes and has restructured itself into teams.

While the employees have gone along with both the TQM and re-engineering initiatives, they have not always been eager to accept the changes in responsibility that have come with these initiatives. Your department in particular has been reluctant to give up the current hierarchical structure.

The time has arrived, however, for the department to change its mindset. The most recent reorganization broke up the department and put people into process teams. First-level supervisors either moved to different assignments or simply became part of a team. Your task now is to get the team to develop its governance structure so that it can manage its work.

What would you do as department head?

Reinforcement: Exercises

OBSERVATION

Using the leadership control continuum in Chapter 3, interview 10 teams and see where they fall on the continuum. Describe the teams' satisfaction with their level of control and the effectiveness of the leadership provided both external and internal to the teams.

1. Variation in level of control observed: _____

_____

2. Teams' general satisfaction with each level of control: _____

_____

3. Evidence you found of effectiveness of external leadership: _____

_____

_____

4. Evidence you found of effectiveness of internal leadership: _____
_____
_____

OBSERVATION

Interview a person from management in an organization that frequently uses teams.

1. How did management decide to begin to use teams as an organizational structure?
_____
_____

2. To what extent did management consider the strategic implications of using teams in the organization?
_____
_____

3. What criteria did the management team use to create teams?
_____
_____

4. How does the management team monitor team effectiveness?
_____
_____

5. Given the information you gathered, what is your evaluation of the organization's likelihood to create high performance teams?
_____
_____

OBSERVATION

Consider the operation of a team in the public view. It could be the management of a public entity, and athletic team, or a community organization.

1. Based on the information you know about that team, write a purpose statement that you think would be appropriate for the team.
_____
_____
_____

2. Given the purpose you have identified, what kinds of goals might be appropriate for that team?

Annual goal: _____

Quarterly goals: _____

                   _____

                   _____

                   _____

3. Develop three measures for one of the goals you developed. Be sure to choose measures that will look at achievement or progress towards the goal from three different perspectives. Make the measures outcome based rather than activity based.

                   _____

                   _____

                   _____

OBSERVATION

Refer to the questions the manager should ask the team when she or he is acting in the role of coach. Talk with a manager who sponsors or coaches a team and see to what extent she or he asks these questions.

1. As a coach, what kind of questions does this manager use in working with his/her team?

_____

_____

_____

_____

2. Given the questions this coach asks, how effective do you think she or he is?

_____

_____

_____

_____

3. From your discussion with the coach, what questions would you add to the list provided in the book?

_____

_____

_____

Developing a Team Process

Learning from this section:

■ To compare and contrast the different phases of team process development.

■ To develop useful team ground rules and adjust them as circumstances change.

■ To define and apply effective participation techniques.

■ To identify and develop effective decision making within a team.

Other things I want to learn about developing effective team processes:

■

■

To state the obvious, the pursuit of teamwork occurs in a forum where people meet and work together to reach agreements and resolve issues. Yet, for all its obvious importance, the most common criticism of teams is that team meetings are a waste of time; discussion is not open and constructive, and decisions are avoided or not supported. How the team operates—its process—is therefore critical to the success of the team.

Developing an effective team process is evolutionary. It begins with the first team meeting and, if the process is effective, continues to evolve and improve. Below is a diagram of the evolution the team process goes through. Note that for an effective team, the process evolves in a circular way, continually renewing into a spiral of increasing performance.

Effective teams go through three basic phases: formation, development, and renewal. In the formation stage, the team does the ground-breaking work of deciding on a task and agreeing to basic rules of operation. The development phase allows the team to make progress toward the task and get comfortable with the meeting process and one another. In the transformation phase, the team uses task information and participant cohesion to move itself into innovation and creative problem solving. The renewal phase allows the team to mature and improve, and it is able to take on more complexity—either within the current task or with a new task. Increased complexity requires the team to reexamine its purpose and process, and the team begins the cycle anew—except on a higher plane. And so the process continues with the effective team growing and developing, able to handle more complex and difficult issues and continuing to add value to the organization.

Between each stage there is a breakpoint (see Figure II.1). These breakpoints represent plateaus that teams commonly reach in their evolution. Teams have a tendency to stall on these plateaus, continually reworking old issues, solutions, and behaviors. To continue to improve, the team must break through the current phase into the next more demanding one.

Phase 1: Formation

DEFINITION

The team begins its evolution at the point of formation. All team members are together for the first time, and their initial task is to define what they want to accomplish and how they will operate as a team. We have discussed the value and method of purposing. We learned that team members need to validate and clarify the reason why they are coming together and what they hope to accomplish. The team then needs to set goals and establish measures to assure both progress and achievement in the team's work. As stressed earlier, teams will benefit if they take the time needed to purpose well, for without a clear task definition the team will not perform well.

FIGURE II.1 Evolution of a Team

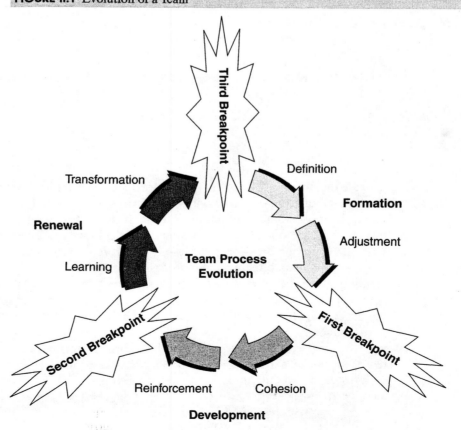

In this section of the book we will discuss process definition for the team. Chapter 4 tells about the importance of ground rules to the effective operation of the team. Ground rules define the way the team will operate. They focus on developing and maintaining relationships with those outside and inside the team, and on principles and procedures for day-to-day functioning of the team. Without these ground rules, the team wastes time and energy, and it is faced with deciding how to do things over and over again. In addition, without ground rules team meetings and activities often result in conflict over misunderstandings in expectations. Clear ground rules give all team members a common platform for participation and decision making.

ADJUSTMENT

The second part of the formation phase is adjustment. Both task goals and process rules tend to be made under a mantle of idealism. As the demands of the task and personalities of team members unfold, the team needs to clarify and adjust its expectations. Task issues at this point tend to revolve around deadlines and the scope of the work. Team members have, by this time, put the team charge in context with their other responsibilities. It is time for a reality check to clarify what the team can accomplish and within what time frames.

Adjustment in ground rules takes on an internal focus. Given that the dates and times of meetings and that initial interaction procedures have been set, the team now becomes concerned with managing internal relationships. Preparation for meetings and the quality and quantity of participation in them are common issues. As leadership within the team begins to develop, power and position struggles are not uncommon. The more the team is structured toward being self-led, the more volatile this period can be since there is not a designated leader to resolve conflict. Tension almost always exists among team members during this adjustment period, for team members are struggling to find their place in a new environment. In fact, tension is so natural that absence of tension should be a cause for concern. It may well indicate that team members have withdrawn or that they are disinterested and unwilling to expend the effort to bring this collection of individuals into a team. Apathy is a more dangerous enemy to the team in this phase than is tension.

The adjustment phase of evolution comes to a breakpoint when the team gets mired down in arguments about what to do and who should do what. When team meetings rehash old issues or when people do not meet their deadlines or keep their promises, blaming becomes the norm. Teams need to push through this adjustment phase. They do this by setting clear *short-term* goals, celebrating early successes, putting ground rules in concrete form with a charter and rituals, and by confronting those who violate the common rules. The break-through strategy, then, is one of clarity and firmness. The team must agree that their charge is serious business and that they will hold themselves and one another accountable for the team's success. If the team does not break through this phase, it will deplete its energy by going in circles. Slowly members will stop attending meetings, and the team will remain a team in name only.

Phase 2: Development

COHESION

For those teams that pass through the formation phase, the next phase is development, which focuses on building cohesion and reinforcing team purpose. Having settled the process disputes and experienced some success, the team is making progress. This phase is characterized by interest and energy.

In the cohesion phase, attention focuses on task, teammates accommodate one another's peculiarities, and the team begins to gel. Team members tend to be supportive of one another's ideas. Ground-rule issues revolve around participation. The team wants to improve its internal processes and to make sure that team members feel accepted. In parallel fashion, task issues deal with work methods. Team members are working together, gathering information, and making decisions in a spirit of cooperation and continuous improvement. Life in the team is good. Team members begin to identify with the team, and team members develop important relationships.

REINFORCEMENT

In the reinforcement stage, cohesion builds and homogeneity increases. Team members take on one another's norms, and getting along becomes very important. Ground rules focus on confidentiality and meeting efficiency—anything to protect against stirring up trouble inside the team. Task issues focus on showing a solid front; agreement assures the right course of action. The team's good ideas are remembered and exaggerated.

Reinforcement leads to the second breakpoint for a team. Unlike the first breakpoint that centered on conflict, this one centers on comfort. As the reinforcement stage evolves, it becomes too much of a good thing. The team at this point tends to isolate itself from outsiders—"*they* just don't understand us." The team is likely to suppress disagreement—"we do not have time to disagree," or "we need to get along." The team often loses perspective—"we do not need more information; ours is the best way." With these attitudes, team development comes to a halt. The team loses energy because there are no new things to do; their investment is in self-preservation and self-perpetuation. If the team stays together, it often takes on a siege mentality—"everyone is out to get the team." The result is that the team closes ranks even more and views outsiders suspiciously. Soon the team is lost in irrelevance as the rest of the organization moves on without them.

Teams must break through this second barrier. Team members do this by using their cohesion to take on new issues and to challenge their current problem-solving methods and assumptions. The team lets its confidence foster exploration rather than solidify its position; it lets its trust encourage diversity in ideas. At this point in team development, task goals need to be stretched, outsiders need to be brought into the team, and process goals need to focus on creativity and exploration. The break-through strategy for the development stage is creating the freedom to explore and to change mindsets.

Phase 3: Renewal

LEARNING

Passing through the second breakpoint, a successful team enters the renewal stage of team evolution. This stage operationalizes the mindset changes that allowed the breakthrough. Since the team is now willing to explore new ways of doing things, it needs to learn new skills. The focus of the team shifts outward, and the new mindset is one of understanding the plethora of issues at hand and embracing the variety of relationships involved in accomplishing its task.

In the learning stage, the team shrugs off the temptation it confronted in the development phase—to reinforce the current way of doing things. The team decides to push beyond its present limits. It may decide to benchmark against a new industry or learn a new technical or process skill. Outsiders become a source of useful information and potential partners, and differing points of view are no longer threatening. Team attention is focused on growing and developing both as individual team members and as a team unit. Positive energy generated in this process brings new comfort and propels the team into developing new ideas and activities, and the team is revitalized. Task assignments take on new life with fresh ideas, and team process becomes more confrontive. Tension in the team returns, but this time it is positive—focused on issues rather than personalities. All this energy is driven by the team for the benefit of the team. Commitment and mutual accountability have become a reality. The team has become high performing, and its potential is awesome.

TRANSFORMATION

Transformation is the final stage in the cycle of team evolution. The team is at a high energy level with creativity and cohesiveness in sync. Meaningful results are coming from the team's actions. True synergy is displayed in the far-sighted, innovative resolutions the team suggests. In fact, the team seems to have more ideas than it knows what to do with. Once again the team has reached a breakpoint. If the team issues remain the same, the team will get bored. The team tires of working in the same arena; there are only so many meaningful variations to a theme. The team needs a new challenge.

The only way to sustain the energy of the learning stage is to stress and press the team. If the team fails to take on more complex challenges, it will slip back to the comfort of the reinforcement stage. To rally a second time from that comfort is very difficult, so the successful team must take the risk of transformation. Transformation requires challenging all that the team has built: its assumptions, its process, and its purpose. This may mean disbanding the team, changing membership, partnering with a former "enemy," and/or taking on controversial issues. Whatever the new challenge is, it will be a significant departure from the past. It will put the team in a new situation with a new mindset. This is the third breakpoint. If the team can change, it can renew itself and continue to achieve on a higher plane.

An example of a team positioned for transition is the process team described earlier in the book. The order entry team chose to form a cross-functional team from the units involved in order entry. They were in a middle-ground position; that is, they were willing to include all members of the order-fulfillment process but were unwilling to include those departments outside order processing, specifically manufacturing and accounting. For this team, if it is able to get through the evolution process in its unit redesign task, its transformation challenge could be to take on the entire product delivery process. Having accomplished the restructuring of one process, they would likely be ready to take on a larger, more complex task. They might even provide that very traditional organization its first venture into a self-led process team!

In their book *Built to Last,* Jim Collins and Jerry Porras talk about organizations that endure. Their research showed that survivors have several things in common, including strong core ideologies, an impatience with the status quo, a willingness to practice self-reflection and to challenge their assumptions, and an eagerness to take on the big issues. "Built to last" companies are confident, risky, robust entities. The same can be said of teams that endure. Core ideologies that include trust, mutual accountability, and commitment drive the team to think well, interact effectively, and take on serious issues. The team's process enables it to grow and develop. The team that pays close attention to process evolution and has the courage to push through breakpoints, has the best chance to reach excellence and to endure.

In this section of the book, we will deal with several aspects of an evolving team process. We will discuss the ground rules that the team must set to define and protect the practices it wants to follow. These ground rules help the team to define itself. Ground rules also provide the mechanism for the team to adjust both its task objectives and progress as well as its process goals.

In the later chapters in this section, we will discuss the rules of participation that help a team balance member contributions. Effective means of participation allow the team to become cohesive. Team members have a forum for sharing their ideas, and support and cooperation are fostered. Once the team has developed a level of trust, participation can allow the team to learn new conservation skills and to draw out multiple perspectives on an issue. Effective participation within the team can build the security needed in the development phase and then permit the break-through into renewal.

Finally, we will explore the key reason for the existence of a team—decision making. For successful teams, decision making is a caldron of controversy, diversity, creativity, and trust. It is not a peaceful process. It is a rough-and-tumble romp into new ideas and risky goals. The tension is high, but so is the camaraderie. To reach this level of effective decision making, the team must mind its process, develop key problem-solving skills, and foster key attitudes on creativity and innovation. In the next three chapters, we will discuss both the methods of effective decision making needed in the development phase and the new thinking needed for the renewal phase.

4

Ground Rules

Learning from this chapter:

■ To identify key process ground rules for meeting management.

■ To develop clear work expectations with team members.

■ To define and discuss issues of confidentiality that cause problems for teams.

■ To be able to develop useful ground rules covering common team process obstacles.

Other things I want to learn about using ground rules for effective team process:

■

■

In this chapter we will discuss three areas where teams need to establish ground rules:

- Meeting management
- Work expectations
- Confidentiality and support

Meeting management rules guide the participation and decision-making process in the team. Work expectations focus on quantity of effort and task responsibility. Expectations around confidentiality and support help the team build the climate necessary for trust, risk taking, and innovation.

Meeting Management

Meetings are the primary forum for the team's work. While meeting management may seem a rather mundane issue for teams, how the team establishes and manages meeting issues will often portend the overall success of the team. The key ground rules for meetings usually address attendance, representation, and information management.

Attendance represents the first opportunity for the team to put into action some of its values and expectations. It is the first opportunity for the team to practice mutual responsibility.

If the member simply cannot attend regularly, then the team needs to decide on a secondary role for that team member or assign a new member.

The first decision the team must make is to define acceptable attendance. Attendance requirements depend on the work and culture of the organization and the requirements of the task. For example, some organizations require their people to travel a great deal. In that situation it is unlikely that the team can require that team members attend every meeting. The team must establish a schedule that allows team members the maximum opportunity to attend and then be clear about what is an acceptable attendance rate. If a team member is not regularly present at team meetings, she or he cannot be an effective team member, certainly not a core team member as described earlier. The team then needs to decide on a secondary role for that team member or assign a new member.

Common questions for team members to ask around attendance include:

- How often will the team meet?
- For how long?
- Where?
- What is tardiness and how should it be dealt with?
- What is the definition of regular attendance?

A more delicate issue of attendance is the notion of what constitutes "being" at the meeting. Some people bring their bodies but not their minds and souls to the meeting. Such team members will bring along other work to do; will constantly leave the room to make phone calls; or will not participate. The team must clearly define what it expects from team members once they arrive at the meeting.

A related problem for teams is tardiness. If members constantly come to the meeting late, it creates a disruption. Sometimes tardiness is a power play for the team member, especially if he or she knows the team waits to begin until the person arrives or that they will repeat what has transpired just for the benefit of the person who is tardy. The guiding principle on attendance is that the team should be careful not to reward poor performance. Team meetings must begin and end within the agreed time frames so that members can plan their own schedules. If team members who are late find that the meeting has begun without them, they are more likely to be on time in the future. If the meeting waits for the person, there is no incentive to come on time. In the same way, if the team is willing to revisit issues once the member has arrived, there is no incentive to be there for the original discussion. Also, when the team revisits an issue for an individual person, that person usually has an increased amount of influence over the topic because that individual has heard only a summarized version of the topic of discussion. It is not uncommon for a late-coming member to challenge a decision and have the team revoke what it had earlier agreed upon. If this team behavior occurs regularly, power-oriented team members will soon use such behavior to manipulate team decisions.

Some people bring their bodies but not their minds and souls to the meeting.

In effective teams, an absent team member respects and values the decisions of the team and feels confident that the team will reach a good decision.

Attendance expectations must be clear and accepted by all team members. It is often helpful for them to write down their expectations so that commitment is clear. To be effective, ground rules have to be specific. To simply say that team members will all participate is too general to evoke a commitment to adherence to the rules. In the Team Charter in the appendix of the book, there is a format that teams can use to record their ground rules.

In addition to setting the ground rules, the team must decide what it will do if a team member does not abide by the rules. It is vital that these ground rules be set at the beginning of team meetings, before transgressions occur. If the team waits until it has to deal with inappropriate behavior, it will not be able to separate the ground rule from the problem person, and resentments are likely to occur.

Enforcement is a very important issue for teams. Addressing ground-rule violations is usually the first opportunity for team members to give one another feedback and to reinforce team values. If the team is unwilling or unable to confront attendance issues, it will not be able to deal with the more challenging decision-making expectations that will arise as the team matures and deals with difficult task issues. Keeping ground rules is the first indication of whether the team is serious about its work.

One of the questions that often arises in relation to attendance in team meetings is whether members should send substitutes to meetings they themselves cannot attend. The current thinking on this question is that they should not send substitutes. While it may be appropriate to send a substitute to a group meeting where people simply report information, it is not appropriate to send a substitute to a team meeting. Each team member plays too intimate a role in the team to suggest that a substitute would be able to take the person's place.

Two underlying concepts lead to this "no substitutes" conclusion, and both are based on trust. In an effective team, the absent member must be able to trust that fellow team members will represent his or her issue in the discussion. In addition, the absent team member must respect and value the decisions of the team and accept that, even though she or he cannot attend, the absent team member feels confident that the team will reach a good decision.

> **The absent member must be able to trust that fellow team members will represent his/her issue in the discussion.**

This question of substitution is so serious for teams that it needs to be addressed specifically and concisely. Some things that successful teams can do to manage this situation are:

- Appoint a specific person on the team to represent and speak for the views of the missing person. During team discussion, the spokesperson will straightforwardly present what she or he thinks the views and values of the missing member would be.
- Create a ground rule that if a person knows he or she will miss a team meeting, he or she must notify the meeting manager. The meeting manager and the person going to be absent decide how to provide the absent member's views to the team.
- Establish a ground rule to identify the key people needed for a specific discussion. If any of those people cannot attend the meeting, it is canceled. If the meeting is canceled regularly, the team must then step back and discuss the issues of purpose and commitment.
- If a member is missing from a meeting, someone on the team is designated to meet with that person before the next meeting to advise the person of the decisions made and the discussion supporting the decision.
- If decisions are made during a meeting from which a member is absent, the team will not revisit the decision when the missing member returns. The team may decide to revisit its decision because of new information, or for any other content reason, but not simply because the missing member may not agree with the decision that was made.

Teams can use any one or a combination of these tactics or come up with ground rules that meet a team's particular needs. The intent of these actions is to make sure that the team makes progress while also accommodating the inevitable absences of team members.

Reflection

Consider a time when you have been with a team since its inception. Reflect on how the team went about establishing ground rules. In the checklist below, indicate which ground rules the team **overtly** addressed (discussed the issue and came to a team agreement on how to handle it) and which the team **covertly** dealt with (no open discussion but the actions of the group over time established the ground rule). Then indicate the effectiveness of that ground rule.

Ground-Rule Process Assessment							
Topic	*NO Ground Rule*	*Covert Ground Rule*	*Overt Ground Rule*	*Effectiveness of Ground Rule*			
Length of meetings	☐	☐	☐	1 2 3 4 5 Not Valuable Valuable			
Tardiness	☐	☐	☐	1 2 3 4 5 Not Valuable Valuable			
Absence	☐	☐	☐	1 2 3 4 5 Not Valuable Valuable			
Level of "being there" at meetings	☐	☐	☐	1 2 3 4 5 Not Valuable Valuable			
Substitution for absent members	☐	☐	☐	1 2 3 4 5 Not Valuable Valuable			
Getting information from absent member	☐	☐	☐	1 2 3 4 5 Not Valuable Valuable			
Getting information to absent member	☐	☐	☐	1 2 3 4 5 Not Valuable Valuable			
Ground rule enforcement	☐	☐	☐	1 2 3 4 5 Not Valuable Valuable			

Team Work

Now apply the ground-rule assessment information to your current team. For the ground-rule topics, respond to the questions below.

Which of the preceding ground rules does your current team effectively use?

_____

_____

_____

Which other suggested ground rules would help your current team improve its process?

_____

_____

_____

How would you approach your team members to encourage them to establish these ground rules?

_____

_____

_____

Team Charter

Record your suggestions, ideas, and decisions in the Team Charter in the appendix of the book.

The final meeting-management issue concerns information management. Information is the gold that the team mines during its meetings. It must be recorded and safeguarded if it is to be valuable. Teams must, therefore, have ground rules and processes for recording, transforming, and distributing meeting information.

The way a team records information both greatly impacts participation and the quality of decisions made and influences those persons external to the group. The focus of our discussion in this chapter will be on internal recording of issues. In Chapter 10, when we discuss politics and the need for an external focus for the team, we will return to this issue of recording and publishing team information.

The team must decide on two recording issues: how to display information for decision making and how to preserve information for recall. Recording decisions made requires a method that will display clearly the good information and ideas that flow from members in an irregular manner throughout a meeting. Many, many good ideas are left unaddressed during team meetings because there is no mechanism for the team to record them. There are several ways for the team to keep track of ideas. One of the most effective is to have a team member play the role of recorder and to keep track of *all* ideas that are brought to the table. This person could also be sure that each person has an opportunity to talk. This role of recorder/facilitator can be played by an outside member, which is often beneficial in the early life of the team. However, over time the team needs to facilitate its own process. The more each team member can develop the skills of listening and understanding the views and ideas of others, the better off the entire team will be. If the team always uses an outside facilitator, the team abdicates its responsibility to learn this key skill as a team.

There are a couple of guidelines that help this recording/facilitating process work well during team meetings. First, the recorder needs to use a public format for recording information, ideas, and decisions. This format needs to be one where everyone can see it and, if necessary, change it. Flip charts, white boards, overhead transparencies, and interactive computer note taking are all possible. The reason for the visual display for all to see is to establish team ownership for the information and to allow the team to recall what has been discussed. Access to minutes kept in the traditional way is limited and delayed, and therefore does not provide useful information for the discussion process.

A second guideline for the facilitator is always to use the exact language of the speaker. It is a temptation for the facilitator to edit the speaker's words if the facilitator thinks she or he can say it better or wants the comment shortened to record it more easily. Resist the temptation! If the comment needs to be shorter, ask the speaker to rephrase it, or if the person is having trouble, ask the rest of the team to provide more concise language. The purpose of recording is understanding, not correct grammar. To keep the ownership of ideas and discussion vested in the team, it is critical to use the team's own words.

A third suggestion is that the recorder be a member of the team who does not have passionate feelings about the issue being presented. The recorder must be sure that all important comments are recorded. If the recorder has a heavy stake in the issue, he or she can influence, by exclusion or editing, the information recorded. If the issue is very controversial for the team, it may be appropriate to bring in an outside facilitator.

Common questions for the team to address about the information recording process include:

- What information from team discussion should we record/preserve?
- How should we record/preserve this information?
- What information should we share with those outside the team? How much? In what format?

Agenda building is another important recording task. Very often the agenda for the meeting is composed in the absence of the team and will therefore only by accident include what the team wants to discuss. The best time to build an agenda for the next

Many, many good ideas go left unaddressed during team meetings because there is no mechanism for the team to record them.

To keep the ownership of ideas and discussion vested in the team, it is critical to use the team's own words.

The recorder needs to use a visible format for recording information, ideas, and decisions.

meeting is at the end of the current meeting. What discussion items do the team members wish to pursue next time? What new information do they want to discuss? Where does the next team meeting fall in their time frame of accomplishment—does something need to be completed by the next meeting?

Like meeting notes, the agenda should be built publicly with people volunteering to do research, gather materials, contact other people, or pursue other activities related to the agenda. With the input of all, each team member knows what will be expected of him or her by the next meeting. If issues that need to be addressed occur after the agenda has been set, the team needs to devise a way to share that information with all members and to decide how to put the item on the agenda.

Some teams leave an open space on the agenda for the inevitable new situation. If no new situation arises, team members can expand the discussion of other issues or they can adjourn. Other teams prioritize agenda items so that if something is to be postponed the person responsible for the agenda can make the adjustments. Operate by the guideline that says that if an agenda item is moved three times, the team must decide how important the item truly is and whether they should just omit its discussion. Effective teams construct agendas carefully and are willing to take the time to address issues that will make their meeting time productive.

Teams must be careful not to confuse meeting structure and efficiency with effectiveness. If meetings seem unproductive, team members often respond by setting time limits on discussion and making rules that do not allow changes in the agenda. Seldom do these efforts result in better meetings. The focus of improvement in meetings needs to center around content and the decision-making process.

For example:

- What issues really need to be discussed?
- What time frame makes sense for the issues the team needs to discuss?
- What meeting format makes sense for the issues the team needs to discuss?
- What information do we need to have a useful discussion?
- Who needs to be present in order for appropriate decisions to be made?

Meetings tend to take on a routine that is often quite unrelated to the work that needs to be accomplished. Teams talk about unnecessary issues but fail to give enough attention to serious issues; membership gets fixed, as does the meeting place and format. Eventually, the team finds itself with a process that seldom meets its needs. The team needs to challenge its meeting process on a regular basis and be willing to change the process to meet the issue rather than force the issue into the prevailing process.

A role the team often assigns on a rotating basis is that of the meeting manager. This person is charged with the administrative tasks of the meeting. This may include completing and distributing an agenda, securing a room and equipment, drafting minutes, inviting needed nonteam members, and other tasks, depending on the meeting agenda. These tasks can be burdensome if they always fall to the same person; rotated, they are easy to handle, and they provide for new ways to address team issues.

A final recording duty is that of drafting the meeting minutes. Most teams find that meeting minutes are extremely valuable. However, to be of value they do not need to be extensive or fancy. For example, if the meeting notes are done carefully on the flip charts, they can be transcribed for meeting minutes. Meeting minutes certainly can be done in outline form. If the team wants members and others to read the minutes, they need to be short, relevant, and easy to understand.

Some creative teams even use mindmaps for meeting notes. Mindmaps are brief, nonlinear descriptions of what took place at the meeting. A mindmap of a meeting of the facility planning team we described earlier might look like Figure 4.1.

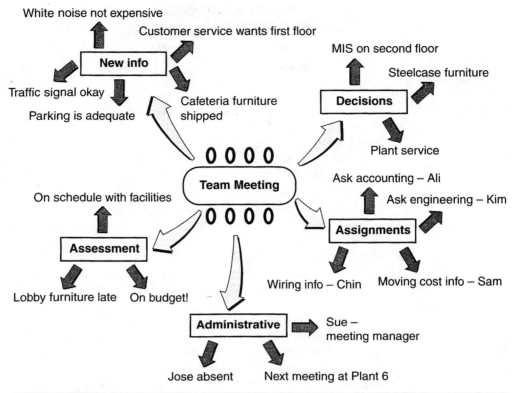

FIGURE 4.1 Example of a Mindmap

If the team wants members and others to read the minutes, they need to be short, relevant, and easy to understand.

Mindmaps are an imaginative way for teams to collect and share information. People reading the mindmap, which is easy to create, get a sense of the dynamics of the meeting. If the team wants the distributed outcome of its meeting to be more formal, the team can still use a mindmap to keep minutes and then translate the mindmap for distribution in a more linear and narrative form. In the exercises at the end of this section there are instructions for drawing a mindmap for a meeting you attend.

Work Expectations

The second area for focus with ground rules is work expectations. People join teams with very different ideas about the work involved in being a member of the team. Few people will deliberately perform poorly, but team members need information about the standards of the team. For example, it is common for people to send out information about the topic of a meeting and then never reach that topic at the meeting or never refer to the information provided. If there is not a positive consequence for meeting preparation, participants will not read materials sent prior to meetings.

On the other hand, some meetings ask for people to give their interpretations, opinions, and recommendations based on the material provided prior to the meeting. In this case, participants are very likely to be prepared. Having had either one of these experiences, or any of the various experiences in between, will define what a team member thinks she or he is accountable for in a team meeting.

Common questions teams address in their ground rules involving work expectations include:

- What is the quality of work expected?
- What is the quantity of work expected?

- How is the timeliness of work defined?
- What does it mean to come prepared to a meeting?

Few people will deliberately perform poorly, but team members need information about the standards of the team.

As an example of setting work expectation ground rules, let's look at a team that has been brought together to put on a three-day conference. The team members know each other, but they are forming a task team rather than a work team since they represent different departments and will disband when the conference is over. This task team has a wide range of positions represented around the table, including two first-level supervisors, three middle managers, two senior managers, and an outside consultant. With this kind of task team, it is likely that the work expectations will be quite different.

The first issue the team needs to address is the quantity of work expected. This is usually done through task assignments. For this team, task assignments include securing facilities, contacting speakers, designing the program, and putting together a list of those to be invited. If the team is to work well, all members must get real work to do. If the two supervisors get all the assignments and the more-senior people just get reports, resentment will be the result. Fortunately, in this example, the senior managers used their experience and contacts to secure speakers for the conference. The work assignments might have been better if the senior managers had worked with a supervisor so that that person would begin to develop the network skills and resources of the senior managers.

Quality of work proved to be a more difficult issue for this team to address. A team of three members was asked to put together a design for the program. One of the team members turned out to have work expectations substantially different from the other two. At the meeting to which this subgroup was to bring a rough draft of their ideas for conference topics and format for discussion with the entire team, two of the members brought in typed, complete ideas. The third member, however, brought in handwritten, incomplete ideas that appeared to have been put together just minutes before the meeting. Information from the first two members had been duplicated so every team member could view their suggestions. The third member had only his personal copy. The result was that the first two parts of the conference were thoroughly discussed and planned. The third part, however, was dealt with only vaguely, and at the end of the conference, it was clear that the third part was the weakest of the conference.

Hindsight makes it clear that two things should have happened in this meeting. When the assignments were handed out, the expectations for product should have been made clear. At this point it would have been easy for a team member to ask what kind of format the team wanted so that each person knew what was expected. The less desirable alternative would have been to address the issue after the information had come to the meeting. The team might have suggested that the third member complete his ideas and bring the finished information to the next meeting, being very specific about how the information was to be provided.

An effective way for ground rules to be reinforced is for the team to reflect regularly on the effectiveness of the current meeting.

Not addressing the issue, which is what this team chose to do, does not help the team grow and develop. The members that provided the complete work resented the member who had arrived unprepared, and the rest of the team members probably judged the person harshly as well. In defense of the third member, he may not have understood what the norm was for draft work. Maybe on other teams, handwritten, vaguely formed ideas were the norm. It is always wise to reaffirm work expectations at both the overall team level and with each assignment. It is better to err on repeating what everyone knows is the level of work expected than to have misunderstandings of expectations.

An effective way for ground rules to be reinforced is for the team to reflect regularly on the effectiveness of the current meeting. For example, at the conclusion of meetings, the team can spend a few minutes reflecting on the work level of the meeting. Did the team address the right issues? Did the team possess sufficient and appropriate information to carry on a useful meeting and make necessary decisions? Was everyone able to give their point of view? Did the team explore rather than immediately judge the ideas brought to the table? Is everyone satisfied with the progress and process of the meeting?

The answers to these questions can help to improve the work of the team. From the answers, the team should identify one thing that went well in the meeting and decide how team members could make sure it becomes common practice. On the other hand, team members should also identify one thing that hampered the team's work and decide how to prevent it from happening again. To restate an earlier conclusion, team work does not work effectively without attention and learning. Successful teams continually monitor their performance and make regular adjustments so that they make improvements before the team has serious problems.

Reflection

Reflect on a time where you were given a team assignment. Describe below how confident you were about the performance expected of you.

Team assignment: _____

Information provided on quantity of work: _____
_____

Information provided on quality of work: _____
_____

Information provided on timeliness of work: _____
_____

Impact of clear or vague information on your performance and confidence:
_____
_____
_____
_____

Team Work

Now transfer this thinking to your current team. Have you and your team members made work expectations clear?

What kind of information do you need to discuss and agree on regarding preparation for meetings?
_____
_____

What kind of information do you need to discuss and agree on regarding quality of work brought to the team?
_____
_____

What kind of information do you need to discuss and agree on regarding quantity of work done by team members? Consider this question from both an equity standpoint and a time standpoint.
_____
_____
_____

Team Charter

Record your suggestions, ideas, and decisions in the Team Charter in the appendix of the book.

Confidentiality

The last issue for team ground rules that we will discuss concerns confidentiality and support. Nothing can destroy trust as quickly in a team than to have team discussions shared with those outside the team. When team members hear summaries of what occurred in the team, they often feel that their comments are misrepresented or misinterpreted or, at the very least, that they would like to speak for themselves. To avoid these problems, team members need to decide how they will represent the meeting discussion to others.

Some teams choose a spokesperson for the team. This is probably wise if the work of the team is both highly complex and highly controversial and if there are specific constituencies that need to receive regular reports. Other teams identify instances when the information they are discussing is confidential and not to be shared outside the team. The expectation is that fellow team members will not share any information on this topic outside the meeting.

As with other ground-rule topics, team members often have very different expectations about confidentiality. Teams, as well as the individual members personally, vary widely in how open they want their discussions to be. Yet it is common for teams to neglect discussing confidentiality until one member has breached the unspoken norm. Dealing with a specific infraction takes the team down the path of accusation and blame, and it is difficult to get back to the guidelines for confidentiality and off the personal conflict. It is necessary to be quite specific when the team sets confidentiality guidelines. It is not sufficient to say that team members should keep the meeting information to themselves. This is too sweeping and presents a dilemma when team member constituents ask questions about the meeting.

To develop useful guidelines the team needs to discuss questions such as the following:

- What topics are to be considered confidential?
- How will team members identify confidential information?
- How should team members treat this information?
- How should team members portray team meetings to outsiders?
- Who should be the spokesperson for the group?
- Who should receive meeting minutes?

The discussion on confidentiality also requires a discussion on enforcement and consequence.

- How will the team address instances where a team member has violated the confidentiality norm?
- What will be the consequence of such an action?

An example of a team that struggled with confidentiality will show the serious impact that these issues can have on team climate and progress. The team in question was charged with designing a new educational program. The team had 10 members drawn from units that would be providing information or presenters to the program. Two of the members were outside the department and were expected to ensure that the new program meshed with other company programs.

The team spent its first few meetings talking about the concepts of the program and how the program was to be implemented. It was agreed that the team wanted to keep the other members of the department aware of its progress. Eventually, the team came to the point of making some decisions about what would be included in the program. Three different models were presented for how the program might be designed. The models were quite different and both the content and delivery of information varied within the models.

As the team discussed the various approaches, it became clear that there was discussion about the various models outside the team. In fact, one unit supervisor wrote a memo to the department head pointedly challenging one of the models on the grounds that his unit would only have a minor representation in the program. One of the outside members came to a team meeting unhappy that he heard that he was the obstacle to accepting one of the models. It was clear the team needed to discuss the issue of confidentiality and information sharing.

While the team had agreed that they wanted to keep members of the department informed, they had not provided a mechanism for doing so. Without a method for providing progress reports, individual team members shared accounts of how the team was doing. Given that each team member had preferences for the content and delivery options being discussed, those accounts were not unbiased. And, given the propensity for people to misunderstand, exaggerate, and add their own opinions, the information about the program development process began to bear little resemblance to what actually occurred in the meetings. In addition, as people outside the team began to take positions, team members were getting pressured from various groups to support one model over another. This pressure led to increasingly hostile team meetings as team members began to take positions and advocate rather than look for ways to build the best program for company needs.

In an effort to preserve both the product and process, the team members came to an agreement on the following ground rules:

1. At the end of each meeting the team would develop a progress report to be distributed to all constituents.
2. The team would immediately develop an options report that set forth the main elements of the three models currently under consideration and that ask all department members for feedback.
3. Once the team came up with a draft program it would hold an open forum to discuss the elements of the proposed program.
4. Outside of the above described information sharing methods, team members would not discuss the different models with outside constituents.

By developing specific methods for dealing with the confidentiality of information, the team was able to protect the support atmosphere of the team. Team members once again felt comfortable voicing opinions, knowing that what they said would remain in the meeting room. By meeting with outside constituencies as a group, the team also developed a sense of mutual accountability for the product and stood together to explain their decisions.

Confidentiality issues are difficult ones for the team to discuss. However, if they are discussed as a regular part of the process of setting ground rules, it is easier for team members to share their views and to set out expectations that will minimize transgressions. If ground rules are clear and agreed to, most people will abide by the rules. If a transgression does occur, the team member is usually contrite and has learned a lesson.

Reflection

Consider your past membership on teams and identify the times when issues over confidentiality caused the team difficulty.

Confidentiality Issues That Cause Team Process Difficulties		
Incident	*Frequency*	*Impact*
Misrepresentation of team discussions to outside constituents	1 2 3 4 5 Rare Frequent	
Badmouthing of individual team members	1 2 3 4 5 Rare Frequent	
Announcing decisions before team statement is made	1 2 3 4 5 Rare Frequent	
Other:	1 2 3 4 5 Rare Frequent	
Other:	1 2 3 4 5 Rare Frequent	

Team Work

Now consider your current team(s). What confidentiality issues do you need to clarify?

❑ The types of information that the team considers confidential.
❑ For public statements, who will speak for the team.
❑ If, and how, difficulties the team is having should be discussed outside the team.
❑ Expectations for personal support of team members outside the team.
❑ How confidentiality breaches will be addressed.
❑ Other:

Team Charter

Record your suggestions, ideas, and decisions in the Team Charter in the appendix of the book.

Developing and coming to agreement around ground rules in a sense gives the team practice in working together. It allows an opportunity for team members to get to know one another before the team must address substantive issues. Ground rules also make it easier for teams to perform effectively. By establishing expectations ahead of time, team members empower one another. An individual member, for example, can decide on the basis of the ground rules whether he or she wants to continue to be a member of the team. The team member is also able to manage his or her own behaviors and schedules to be an effective member. Clarifying how the team will operate sets a tone for mutual accountability and individual responsibility that will serve the team well as it moves to decision making and interacting with external forces in the organization.

5

Participation

Learning from this chapter:

■ To compare and contrast different levels of communication in a group.

■ To understand and be able to use verbal behaviors to improve the quality of conversation in the team.

■ To understand the role of contributor on the team.

■ To describe the key participation problems teams face and understand ways to resolve these problems.

Other things I want to learn about effective participation within a team:

■

■

In this chapter we will talk about several dimensions of effective participation. We will begin our discussion with a look at the process of conversation. The art of meaningful conversation is developing as a specific discipline that combines both conversation and thinking skills. Though the discipline is a relatively new one, there are some key principles that apply to teamwork. In that regard, we will take a specific look at the process of conversation and at some of the verbal behaviors used in skillful team communication. It *does* matter how and what you say during team discussion. Effective teams learn to use process and language that draws out relevant information and sets a tone of collaboration.

This discussion will then lead us to a portrait of a key team role, that of contributor. Given the tendency in high performance teams to share leadership, knowing how to contribute to the team process becomes an essential role. In high performance teams, every member accepts responsibility for the entire team process. We will define several different participation roles that must be present for a team to work well.

Conversation

As teams come together and meet, conversation is the primary vehicle that team members use to express their opinions and come to agreement. Nonverbal behaviors are also important in team meetings, and as we increase our use of electronic messages

It does matter how and what you say during team discussion.

through e-mail and bulletin boards, written communication will become important to team meetings. However, because of its significant impact, our discussion here will focus on the internal verbal interactions that the team engages in, namely conversation. In Chapter 6 on decision making we will again discuss some verbal behaviors; but then our focus will be on developing effective thinking and decision making rather than on conversation. In Part IV on politics we will discuss conversation skills with those outside the immediate team with the additional verbal behaviors used in that influencing process.

Conversation skills can be represented on a continuum where interaction among participants includes debate, discussion, and dialogue (see Figure 5.1). For effective team participation and conversation, the team needs to concentrate on the dialogue/discussion end of the continuum.

DEBATE

Many team members come to the conversation table thinking that the purpose of team interaction is to choose one course of action and often to convince the rest of the team that his or her course of action is the "correct" one. In debate, the purpose of the conversation is to "win" the argument through an abundance of evidence or force of logic. Each person on the team pursues the case for his or her position, fending off opposing positions and arguments. Team members listen to each other primarily for the purpose of forming defensive arguments against the other person's statement, and they often do not hear the other person's issues in their entirety.

The goal of the debater is to prevail.

Interrupting and attacking the ideas of the other person is the norm in a debate situation. In a tightly controlled environment, these attacks may stay focused on ideas, but in team meetings where there are few controls, debate often ends in people attacking one another with personal injury and bitterness the outcome.

In debate, compromise (or changing one's position) is not a desired end. The main focus in a debate is to present one's own ideas in such a forceful way as to defeat the ideas of others. The goal of the debater is to prevail.

The reason why understanding the debating philosophy and process is important to teams does not lie in its usefulness but in its pervasiveness. Much of the public discussion people witness revolves around debate, and it is easy for people to think that this is what "conversation" is all about. Seldom do we observe other kinds of team interaction where issues are explored, options generated, and agreement reached. Unfortunately these more useful forms of interaction tend to be less entertaining, and are therefore more often private affairs.

Some common and visible examples of debate include:

Political debates In this forum, both sides engage in trying to convince the listener that their position is the right one; neither side is interested in listening to the other's view; the practice of

---

FIGURE 5.1 Team Conversation Continuum

CLOSED		X OPEN
Debate	**Discussion**	**Dialogue**
Focus is on defending and winning	Focus is on persuading, prioritizing, and deciding	Focus is on exploring and understanding ideas and people

constantly repeating your own position, in more and more extreme form, is common.

Legal processes   With the recent introduction of television into the court-room and the media's fascination with trials, the public is once again exposed to a public debate. In the adversarial legal system, winning is clearly the goal and discrediting the other side the method. Interrupting and attacking are the norm, interrogation the medium.

Issue forums   Whether it be local public hearings, school board meetings, or national talk shows, an issue forum usually encourages people to debate—to focus on their own position and attack the positions of others—rather than try to understand the position of the other side. In fact, we often structure these forums to allow for only one-sided input; there is no intent to reach common agreement. In talk shows, if we can bring people to blows, the ratings go up.

There is some role for debate in our thinking, and there may be some intellectual benefit to its requisite verbal calisthenics, but within debate there certainly is no demonstration of seeking understanding or agreement, or of a willingness to work together—all of which are vital to team work.

The reason why understanding the debating philosophy and process is important to teams does not lie in its usefulness but in its pervasiveness.

As a model for team interaction, debate is generally dysfunctional. Team members often recognize the inappropriateness of debate at the intellectual level. However, since many team members' verbal habits are developed or influenced by exposure to the debate process, debate is often displayed in team meetings. Effective teams seek to minimize debate behaviors at team meetings through ground rules and also work to develop the alternative skills of discussion and especially of dialogue.

DISCUSSION

Discussion is the most common kind of team communication. The word discussion has a root meaning that indicates a process of breaking things apart. Discussion, therefore, focuses on gathering various pieces of information and points of view and analyzing them as discreet items. Team members present their ideas and opinions to fellow team-mates who react to them. Discussion is an important activity for a team, but it is not an end unto itself.

Discussion usually does not generate the level of attack found in debate. Rather, the focus of the conversation tends to be on persuasion. A person using the discussion approach tries not so much to discredit the other side as to convince others that his or her views or ideas are better. The focus, however, remains on one's own position, though the conversation is not as negative as in debate. Passing judgment continues to be a fundamental characteristic of discussion, just as it is in debate. In discussion, the judgment comes in the form of "yes, but" rather than "you are wrong," but it is still judgment. Team members start with the premise that they are right and that it is their job to bring others to their side.

Team members start with the premise that they are right and that it is their job to bring others to their side.

Discussion does allow a person to amend his or her position, but any modification is usually done for the sake of agreement rather than of embracing a new idea. An underlying assumption in discussion is that for agreement to take place, everyone gives up something—a compromise is always the end result. Problems in discussion arise because in most team situations that compromise is not balanced. It is often the same people who give the most to the compromise, and soon they learn it is better not to engage in the discussion at all. This is the situation when you hear the chair or leader of a team say, "I ask team members for their ideas and opinions, but they do not speak up." Chances are, over time, team members have learned that there is little reason to speak up; they are seldom heard, and their ideas rarely prevail.

A primary difficulty teams have in the discussion process is the ability to comprehend all the ideas that surface. Discussion generates many ideas, but most die a death of neglect. Since everyone is pushing his or her own idea, the ideas of those with position power, verbal skills, or persistence tend to survive, but the comprehensive whole of the issue often does not. The ideas that survive are not necessarily the best ideas, nor does the discussion process ensure support for the ideas that remain on the table. Those not willing or able to engage in the heat of the discussion often withdraw both their ideas and their support. The team then is disappointed that the great amount of time expended in discussion did not result in new ideas or in a sense of mutual accountability. That is asking too much of discussion, which generates a collection of ideas, opinions, and options, but little in the way of integration or understanding of those ideas. If the team only engages in discussion, people are encouraged to share information and ideas, but there is neither intention nor any mechanism for exploring those ideas or reaching agreement.

DIALOGUE

To be effective, teams need to temper and interlace their discussions with dialogue. Dialogue is the term Bill Issacs from MIT's Dialogue Project uses to describe effective collective thinking by a group of people. He explains that during the dialogue process, people learn to think together, not just in the sense of analyzing a shared problem or creating shared knowledge, but in truly collective thought where feelings, ideas, and collective actions belong not to one individual, but to all of the team together.

To develop the ability to engage in dialogue, the team must learn to pursue a process of inquiry and open exchange.

To develop the ability to engage in dialogue, the team must learn to pursue a process of inquiry and open exchange. Team members must take the time to explore each aspect of the issue they are facing and to exchange different and even conflicting and provocative information. Exploring the views of team members is a process characterized by deliberate inaction. That is, dialogue is not intended to come to a conclusion. The purpose is not to evaluate or to decide. It is simply to understand. The team steps back and thinks about what the issue means, what its context is.

The goal, then, of the dialogue process is understanding. During the conversation the team members try to learn about the other person's ideas and issues. Most important, they suspend judgment about the "rightness" or "value" of the idea and just try to understand it. This is not an easy process for a team to learn. Our training and instincts urge us to make judgments; to consider ideas good or bad, more valuable or less valuable. We want to eliminate, prioritize, and choose. Yet, all of these are outside the realm of dialogue. The purpose is to listen, understand, and develop a common basis with the team for understanding.

Why is it important that a team go through this period of seeming inertia? To build the foundation for future action. Think of the team discussion process as a triangle. Dialogue forms the base of the triangle that supports discussion and decision making (see Figure 5.2). The broader the base of common understanding, the more discussion and decision making the team can engage in. Without that base, decision making and discussion do not support each other or the team.

We have discussed the strength of discussion and communication in the team before and called it robustness. Dialogue makes a team robust. It allows the team to deal with more and more complex issues and rebound from mishaps. A basis of common understanding allows team members to address one another's concerns when a member is absent and to represent the team to outside constituencies. Common under-

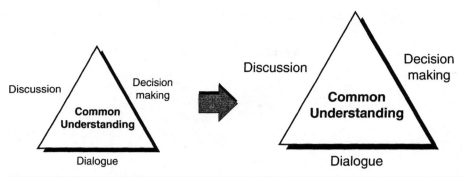

FIGURE 5.2 The Beneficial Impact of Increasing Dialogue

standing also gives the team the base of trust and confidence to suggest new ideas and to take risks.

Being able to dialogue effectively is critical for teams in today's fast-paced environment. Decisions need to be made both quickly and thoughtfully. Dialogue allows the team to deal with this paradox. Unless a team regularly engages in dialogue it will not be able to respond to urgent issues in a wise, timely, and cohesive manner.

Let's use a familiar comparison as an example. When Johnson & Johnson responded to evidence of tampering with its product Tylenol, it was able to set a course of action within hours, if not minutes, of learning of the crisis. The leadership of Johnson & Johnson had a history of dialogue and had discussed company values at great length. Customer safety was an articulated, fundamental company value. Based on the understanding of this value held by the management team, the decision to recall was a quick and easy one. Since the team had already discussed the relationship of cost to customer safety, there was no need to engage in further discussion at the time of crisis. The team knew what to do, and a swift, cohesive decision consistent with organizational values resulted. Everyone on the team understood and supported the decision.

Compare this decision process with Exxon's during the Valdez crisis. Exxon had not done the dialogue necessary to understand both company values and top management perspectives. In the days following the oil spill, Exxon made several false starts at resolution. Messages coming from the company portrayed confusion and often contradictory approaches to resolving the issue. In a time of urgency, the management team had to take time to learn where it stood on fundamental issues. Not only is this kind of delay catastrophic, but the conversations during a time of crisis are likely to be tense and abbreviated. Teams who do not dialogue as a regular part of their team process are likely to make unwise decisions in urgent situations. In addition, they are likely to miss opportunities because of the inability to respond quickly to unplanned-for situations.

An analogy used by David Bohm, a pioneer in the discipline of dialogue, to describe the dialogue process is that of a laser as compared to ordinary light. Putting that analogy in a team context, we can think of regular team discussion as being like ordinary light. It is incoherent and goes in many different directions. While it sheds light, it is not able to build up intensity. Now compare this ordinary light to a laser. Lasers have a coherent, intense beam of light. The light waves build up strength because they are going in the same direction. Lasers can penetrate all kinds of surfaces that ordinary light cannot. So it is with teams. Teams focused in a common direction are capable of acting beyond common expectation. The force for that capability comes from a complete understanding of one another, the organization and the issues at hand. The process for achieving that understanding is dialogue. Discussion is the ordinary light of conversation—a struggle of different ideas that cannot be focused in a unified

TABLE 5.1   Team Conversation Characteristics

Characteristics	Debate	Discussion	Dialogue
Listening	To defeat	To persuade	To understand
Judgment	Absolute conviction of correctness of own position	Acknowledges value of others' positions	Suspends judgment
Presentation	Telling	Selling	Asking
Agreement	Not possible; forced	Ultimate goal; compromise	Not necessary; multiple positions possible
Focus	Attack person and ideas	Change others' positions	Draw out values and positions from others
Process	Repeat and reinforce own position	Bring all positions out on table	Explores issues without taking positions

direction. Dialogue is the laser that allows the team to penetrate complex problems and move forward with clarity.

Table 5.1 compares the different characteristics of team conversation in the debate, discussion and dialogue format. Each format brings useful information to the table, but the discussion and dialogue formats make it much easier to deal with that information and to translate it into a useful decision-making process. Teams generally need to unlearn their debate behaviors and develop the dual conversation skills of discussion and dialogue.

Verbal Behaviors

As previously stated, effective participation within teams does not just happen. The previous section talked about creating a discussion and dialogue context for participation. This section will discuss specific verbal behaviors team members can use to engage in discussion and dialogues and to improve the effectiveness of participation.

Verbal behaviors describe the language practices that people use. As in any other performance arena, the more skill the performers possess and use, the higher the quality of the product. In conversation, verbal behaviors represent that performance skill. Below are five verbal behaviors that teams can use to improve participation at team meetings and activities:

- Set context
- Ask questions
- Use support statements
- Seek out different perspectives
- Share feelings

Set context: Provide information on how the discussion will proceed

This verbal behavior helps people plan their contributions to team conversation. For example, if the team decides that the first step in discussing an agenda item is for each person to identify the key issues to be addressed, team members will come prepared and will wait until all members have brought forth their issues before beginning the discussion. When the team member knows the process by which issues will be addressed, she or he can present ideas at appropriate times and avoid sidetracking the discussion. In addition, if a person presents information that is not suited to the discussion at hand but is relevant to the overall topic, the team can decide where to put this information or when to return to it as the discussion continues.

When a person sets the verbal context of the discussion, she or he suggests a process for discussion. Examples of setting context are:

"Let's gather any new information we have on the issue before we begin our discussion."

"Let's spend the morning discussing issues and then break for lunch. After lunch we can come back and formulate our recommendations."

"The purpose of this meeting is simply to explore the issue and determine what additional information we need. We won't make any decisions until we have that information."

Setting context is a very important part of serious conversation. Until the team deals with the context of a conversation, it has difficulty dealing with the substance of that conversation.

Ask questions: Draw out information from team members

Perhaps the most important verbal behavior that encourages individual participation is asking questions. Questioning provides a method for drawing out both factual information and feelings from team members. However, to obtain the benefits of questioning, the asking must be done well. The most fruitful questions are open-ended ones. Open-ended questions (who, how, tell me) allow the responder to share his or her thinking and feelings about the topic rather than just provide a yes or no response. Often the reasoning behind a person's answer is much more useful than the answer itself. When team members understand one anothers' perspectives, it is easier to find resolutions that will be supported by the entire team. If the team only knows the position the person takes (i.e., "I cannot go along with that."), there is little opportunity for agreement.

Questions that are used to draw team members out need to be based in curiosity, not in challenge. However, developing an effective questioning technique is not easy. Most of the experience we have in asking questions lies at opposite ends of a continuum (see Figure 5.3), and neither extreme is very helpful in team participation.

On one end of the continuum are questions used in therapy situations. These questions tend to be general in nature and to encourage the person to talk at length primarily about his or her feelings. There is little attempt in therapy to direct the discussion or to challenge the accuracy of statements.

At the other end of the continuum are questioning techniques used in interrogation. Here questions tend to be very directed and often close-ended (yes/no) with a tone of hostility. The purpose of interrogation is to uncover truth with little interest in preserving the relationship.

FIGURE 5.3 Questioning Continuum

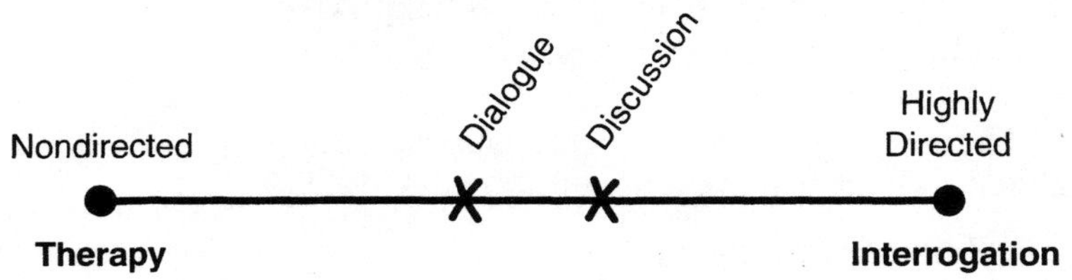

Questioning behaviors useful to team members fall between these two extremes. During dialogue the team needs to be nearer the therapy end of the continuum with a focus on understanding the view of the person being questioned. But even within dialogue, most teams have subject matter they want to focus on rather than just dwelling on general perspectives of team members. In addition, team questioning revolves around building an understanding of collective thought, not around delving into deep personal issues. Therefore, dialogue questions need to be exploratory and nonjudgmental but focused on the issues at hand.

Questioning behaviors that would elicit dialogue include:

"What are the relationships we have developed with the other division?"

"If we were to take the position of merging with the other company, what would you say to your staff?"

"Outsourcing is becoming a common cost reduction option. How do we feel about outsourcing for our organization?"

Discussion questions lean somewhat more to the interrogation end of the continuum. That is, questions are open-ended but directed toward gaining specific information. While the team wants to maintain its nonjudgmental mindset for as long as possible, there is a point in discussion where choices need to be made. Here questions may ask for opinions and commitments, and therefore they are more judgmental and frequently more stress-producing than in dialogue. As the team's use of questions moves toward the interrogation end of the continuum, it is very important that questioning does not take on the hostile tone of the typical interrogation process. Using hostile questions or a condescending tone of voice will shut down all conversation.

"What might be the advantage of opening a new branch office in Paris?"

"How difficult would it be for us to move the relocation timetable ahead by six months?"

"The article in the paper yesterday on our hazardous materials disposal practices was not very positive. How should we respond?"

A final comment about the use of questions may seem obvious and trivial, but in fact it is often a major obstacle to effective questioning. Once a team member asks a question, she or he needs to wait for the answer. Answering one's own question is a common occurrence in conversation. Perhaps this response comes from debate training where questions are often rhetorical and simply used to set a platform for the person to continue talking. Perhaps the response comes from people's general discomfort with a lull in the conversation. Whatever the basis, a long pause at the end of questions will go far in encouraging people to respond and participate.

Use support statements: Positively respond to contributions from fellow team members

Another verbal behavior that improves participation is using support statements. To encourage people to speak up, the conversation climate must be nonthreatening. In a supportive climate, team members acknowledge good ideas, value information provided by fellow team members, and credit team members by name for their contributions whenever possible.

Supporting verbal behaviors must be both overt and specific to establish an open climate for participation. Examples might be:

"I like Angela's idea to work with the San Francisco office to share marketing costs." vs. "Good idea."

"I think we could make that idea work without a great deal of expense." vs. "Okay."

"Last week Amanda brought in the equipment cost figures. They were really helpful to my understanding our problem." vs. "Some of the information we have is useful."

While these examples may seem simple, recognition for contribution sends a strong message to team members that they are valued. The more valued the team member feels, the more commitment she or he is willing to make to team goals and the more sense of accountability team members have to one another.

Seek out different points of view: Consciously draw out the perspectives of other team members

Too much agreement is often a liability for teams. If team members are focused on getting along, they may be reluctant to question the statements of teammates or challenge the team process. Therefore, the team needs to make a special effort to uncover the different perspectives held by team members. If the team establishes a clearly articulated ground rule for seeking out different points of view as a fundamental process and value, team members will be more willing to express an opinion that goes against the grain of the current thinking. Making the process of drawing out different perspectives a common and structured team activity helps to keep the discussion focused on the different aspects of an issue and not on those who are presenting them. Some examples of comments used by successful teams to draw out perspectives include:

"We have two different viewpoints on the table. Let's try for at least two more."

"Sven and Maria, we have not heard from you. What are your thoughts on this matter?"

"What do you think the branch office would say about this idea?"

"Someone take the role of the client and respond to this idea."

A general assumption that people will say what is on their minds is not sufficient; neither does making participation a ground rule work. Effective teams develop specific ways to seek out perspectives. Those teams directly ask for other points of view; they redirect questions and statements to other team members; and they frequently ask quiet team members to comment on specific issues.

Share feelings: Telling team members intuitive instincts or beliefs about information, ideas, or practices within the team

Many teams pride themselves on being rational, logical thinkers. Yet we know that the vast majority, if not all, of our decisions are based on values and emotions. Herbert Simon, the 1979 Nobel Prize winner for economics, suggested that at least 90 percent of the decisions managers make are ethical or value-based. That is, while the decisions appear to be objective, or factually based, the choice and interpretation of information are based on values. Whatever the exact percentage, it is clear that feelings play an important role in the conversation and decision-making processes.

At the same time, our culture can be quite wary of emotion. Team members are often reluctant to share feelings for fear of appearing "soft" and being challenged to produce the facts that support their feeling statements. If the team member's point of view was based strictly on facts, it would not be a feeling; and so the team member is caught in a trap. For example, if a team member shares his or her feelings based on years of experience but does not have convincing facts to support it and is therefore told that the information is not substantive, the team will lose valuable input. Teams must find ways to draw out and identify statements of feeling so the team understands the emotional context of the conversation and the issue.

Sharing feelings is a verbal behavior critical to the dialogue process. If team members do not understand the feelings behind member statements and positions, they will not be able to craft agreements. Commitment to implementing a recommendation is closely linked with my emotional support of that idea.

Teams can effectively share feelings using language like:

"Before we begin to analyze the information we have collected, let's get our intuitive reactions to the proposal out on the table."

"I am feeling uneasy about the path we are taking. I think we should run it by legal counsel before we proceed."

"I am comfortable with the data we now have. It seems to give us the complete picture."

"I am fearful that this idea will meet great resistance when it reaches the shop floor. How do the rest of you feel?"

If feeling statements are directed toward the issue at hand and are not simply general feelings that cloud the issue, they are not only easier to draw out but often more useful in the decision-making process. Teams need to be careful not to challenge feelings. They are meant to be explored and understood. Unlike facts, they are neither right nor wrong. They simply add to the context of the issue. Teams who can incorporate feelings into their conversations enrich their understanding of issues and increase their robustness.

The verbal behaviors we have discussed above come together to form a pattern that allows and encourages participation within the team. As we have said before, bringing a team together is not an easy task. Team members need a feeling of emotional safety within the team for them to share ideas. To the extent that the team uses language that enhances those feelings of safety, the team will be able to tap the potential of team members.

Reflection

Reflect on team meetings you have attended in the past and evaluate how effectively team members used verbal behaviors.

Team being assessed: _____

Verbal Behavior	Frequency of Use			Impact on Team
	Seldom	Sometimes	Often	
Set context				
Ask questions				
Use support statements				
Seek different perspectives				
Share feelings				

Team Work

Now, consider your current team.

What verbal behaviors are absent from your current team meetings?

_____   _____

_____   _____

How would adding these behaviors help the team?_____

_____

_____

What negative verbal behaviors do you see your team using? _____

_____

_____

How might you minimize the use of these behaviors?_____

_____

Team Charter

Record your suggestions, ideas, and decisions in the Team Charter in the appendix of the book.

Contributor Skills

Effective participation is the responsibility of each and every member of the team. Using positive verbal behaviors is a method for encouraging effective participation. Developing contributor skills is where the mutual accountability for participation and the associated verbal behaviors come together. Discussing the skills of contributor will help team members understand and manage their contributions to the team.

Contributor skills refer to the set of behaviors necessary to move a team forward as collective problem solvers. Contributor skills allow all members to be responsible for team process and progress rather than relying only on the team leader to motivate and manage the team. In Chapter 1 we discussed the skill mix to seek in building a team. Contributor skills expand on those skills and allow a holistic view of skill acquisition for the team.

It is clear that a team lacks contributor skills when team members are heard leaving a meeting saying that not much was accomplished; that they do not support the decisions made; or that they feel they were not listened to. To expect one person, chair, leader, or facilitator to be accountable for the meeting process and outcomes is both unreasonable and counterproductive. If teams are to be effective, each member must be responsible for total team action. If a team meeting has deteriorated, each member must attempt to bring the team back to focus. If the team is not providing for adequate input, each team member must call for more participation and information. If the team is not making decisions the team can support, each team member must challenge the decision-making process.

Some of the key contributor skills that need to be learned by team members include:

Initiation	Draw out information and suggestions from the team; clarify direction; move ideas to action.
Energize	Invigorate the team by showing enthusiasm for team tasks; significantly engage in team process and evidence commitment to personal and team role in task achievement.

Organize	Suggest structure and process for the team to follow; bring the group back into focus as work progresses.
Build relationships	Recognize and give value to the contributions of others; strive to be inclusive rather than exclusive.
Be receptive to change	Deal with issues in an open-minded manner; allow self to be persuaded; consider ideas outside current mindset.
Learner	Develop member skills; identify learning needs; take on tasks that heighten personal and team competency levels.

Building contributor skills is key to developing robust teams. The fact that skills are not vested in one person but rather are the domain of the group allows the team to change membership without suffering a serious gap in team competency. With each member possessing all key skills, the team is able to follow many parallel paths in pursuing resolutions to issues. Both of these abilities are essential if teams are to be successful in today's dynamic environment. As stated earlier, organizations do not have time to create stable teams that sequentially pursue one problem-solving alternative after another. Contributor skills give teams the flexibility to consider a variety of options.

Reflection

Think of a team whose process has been going on for some time, whose members you know and have observed interacting.

How well did this team use contributor skills? How many team members were able to use each skill?

Contributor Skills	Skill Use	Effectiveness	Who Can Use Skill?	Improvement Needed
Initiate	☐ Seldom ☐ Sometimes ☐ Frequent	☐ Awkward ☐ Inconsistent ☐ Skilled	• • • •	
Energize	☐ Seldom ☐ Sometimes ☐ Frequent	☐ Awkward ☐ Inconsistent ☐ Skilled	• • • •	
Organize	☐ Seldom ☐ Sometimes ☐ Frequent	☐ Awkward ☐ Inconsistent ☐ Skilled	• • • •	
Build relationships	☐ Seldom ☐ Sometimes ☐ Frequent	☐ Awkward ☐ Inconsistent ☐ Skilled	• • • •	
Embrace change	☐ Seldom ☐ Sometimes ☐ Frequent	☐ Awkward ☐ Inconsistent ☐ Skilled	• • • •	
Learn	☐ Seldom ☐ Sometimes ☐ Frequent	☐ Awkward ☐ Inconsistent ☐ Skilled	• • • •	

Team Work

Now consider your current team.

Which of the contributor skills are now competently used in the team?

_____   _____

_____   _____

How could these be enhanced or sustained? _____

_____

Which of the contributor skills are not being competently used in the team?

_____   _____

_____   _____

How could these be learned and made part of common team process?

_____

_____

Team Charter

Record your suggestions, ideas, and decisions in the Team Charter in the appendix of the book.

Engaging in meaningful conversation needs to be a core competency for an effective team. Meaningful conversation requires good thinking, open discussion, and equivalent participation by team members. At the same time, participation issues are difficult for teams to deal with. By using the ground rules discussed in Chapter 4 and the skills described in this chapter, the team can focus on the process rather than the person. By clearly defining and frequently monitoring participation, the team can learn and course correct before disputes arise and the relationships within the team are permanently damaged. If the purpose of the team is the driving force for action, the participation is the spirit. Effective participation allows the team to gel and capitalize on its many talents.

6

Decision Making

Learning from this chapter:

- Define and discuss the various types of decisions that teams make.

- Identify and know the key steps in the decision-making process.

- Describe and discuss how different states of thinking impact the decision-making process.

- Know the verbal behaviors that help a team become effective at group decision making.

Other things I want to learn about teams and decision making:

-
-

Decision making is at the core of team performance. It is often the very reason for the team's existence, and the degree to which the team has an effective decision-making process is the degree to which the team is successful.

Decision making is at the core of team performance.

In this chapter we will look at the team decision-making process from several perspectives. First, we will discuss the overall process of decision making and how it specifically impacts team performance. For each of the key steps in the decision-making process—generating ideas, discussion, and choice of action—we will discuss specific techniques that can improve each aspect of the process. In the section on generating ideas, we will assess three different approaches to brainstorming that teams might use to improve the number of options the team considers. The section on discussion will consider two ways to improve the quality of team decision making. First, we will look at different kinds of thinking that draw out innovative ideas and resolutions, and then we will describe the verbal behaviors that help the team move effectively through the discussion process. For the third part of decision making—choice of action—we will look at two very different approaches to deciding—justified decision making and consensus—and discuss the advantages and disadvantages of each.

That we bring teams together to solve problems itself suggests that the problems the team is charged to address are complex. Otherwise, we would have had an individual make the decision. This is especially true in a culture that prizes individualism and is relatively suspicious of teamwork. Therefore, it is critical to team effectiveness that the team develop a core competency in decision making. It is not enough that the team understands the process. It is not enough that the team generally applies the principles of effective decision making. Decision making is the most critical function of the team, and it needs focused and constant attention to be done well.

Types of Decisions

The first issue that the team needs to address in the decision-making process is which decisions it will make. There are two considerations here. The first is to identify the type of decision so that the appropriate process can be used, and the second is to decide if that decision is within the charter and purpose of the team.

The matrix in Figure 6.1 shows four major categories of decisions the team will face. Decisions will fall on a continuum between minor and major, and their focus will move from task to people. Depending on where the decision falls, the team needs to develop the appropriate decision-making process. In the next section we will look at the common flow of decision making. The matrix helps the team understand how much time and effort to spend in each of the steps in the matrix and which activities to emphasize.

Teams, like individuals, tend to make all decisions using the same decision criteria and process. The result is that some decisions are made inappropriately. If team decision making focuses on efficiency, then major task and people decisions tend to be less thoughtful than necessary. If, on the other hand, the team decision-making process tends to be contemplative, minor decisions are overassessed and the team is plagued with analysis paralysis. For today's environment, teams need a decision-making process sophisticated enough to differentiate the requirements of different types of decisions.

The upper lefthand corner of the matrix in Figure 6.1 shows what the team needs to consider in making decisions that are characterized as minor task decisions. These decisions tend to be the daily, operations-driven decisions of the team. Examples might be how to collect data for decision making, who to invite to a team meeting, the format for presenting team recommendations or decisions, or when to perform a particular part of an overall activity. The critical point with decisions in this quadrant is time frame. This is the quadrant where decisions can get bogged down. These decisions often represent the concrete aspects of the team's charter, that is, issues the team can readily grasp and deal with. As such, there is a great tendency for the team to spend an inordinate amount of time on these issues. However, these issues need to be resolved quickly so that the team can deal with the more substantive, albeit more difficult and ambiguous, issues.

The upper right quadrant of Figure 6.1 also deals with minor issues, but these tend to be more people-based than task-based. These decisions would include subgroup assignments, attendance and tardiness issues, and team recommendations that have an impact on human resource practices. As with minor task decisions, a key to effectiveness is timeliness. The liability in this decision area is that the team will decide to "reinvent the wheel," redeciding things already covered by policy and practice. While it is true that policy and practice need to be continually challenged, a brief check on the current relevancy of the policy should be sufficient for this level of decision. For this reason, the thinking required in this quadrant is mainly procedural and includes support from constructed thinking since the addition of people into a problem always adds ambiguity. Because these issues involve people, the team needs to consider the impact of the decision on others. Since the decision is at the practice level rather than

<table>
<tr><td colspan="2" align="center">Task   *Focus*   People</td></tr>
<tr>
<td>

Requires decision but has no lasting effect on team or organization.

Time Frame: Fast

Quality: Acceptable

Thinking: Primarily procedural

Process:
1) Identify issue
2) Review facts
3) Consider choices
4) Decide
5) Move on

</td>
<td>

Important to individual but relatively unimportant to organization/team.

Time Frame: Fast

Quality: Consistent

Thinking: Procedural with some constructed

Process:
1) Identify issue
2) Consider current policy
3) Consider impact on others
4) Decide
5) Communicate decision and rationale

</td>
</tr>
<tr>
<td>

Has long-term implications for the organization/team.

Time Frame: Moderate

Quality: Accuracy and acceptance

Thinking: Constructed supported by procedural

Process:
1) Identify issue
2) Gather comprehensive information
3) Search for options
4) Evaluate options
  a. consistent with goals
  b. possible side effects
5) Consult those affected
6) Decide
7) Advise those affected
8) Follow up during implementation

</td>
<td>

Has impact on entire work group.

Time Frame: Long

Quality: Involvement and acceptance

Thinking: Primarily constructed

Process:
1) Involve those affected
2) Gather information on facts and feelings
3) Develop options
4) Consider options carefully
  a. consistent with values/principles
  b. possible side effects
5) Decide
6) Communicate clearly and widely
7) Follow up with learning and development

</td>
</tr>
</table>

The left axis is labeled **Impact**, ranging from **MINOR** (top) to **MAJOR** (bottom).

FIGURE 6.1 Team Decision-Making Matrix

the policy level, the primary concern for the team rests with consistency; that is, the team needs to be sure that it is applying the same criteria and standards to the decisions that fall in this quadrant.

Major task decisions occupy the lower left corner of the matrix (Figure 6.1). These decisions tend to involve the major goals of the team. Examples of decisions that belong in this category include deciding which options the team should recommend or pursue; making major equipment purchases; and choosing the type of market research to engage in. The implications of these decisions are great, and the decision process is primarily focused on the quality of the decision. Because issues with long-term implications offer the organization an opportunity for innovation, the thinking style for the decision needs to be constructed. However, since the decision is primarily technical, there also needs to be a heavy procedural component to the thinking. Decisions in this quadrant lend themselves to analysis, but the team does not want to use only current mindsets to frame that analysis. Major task decisions offer a true payback for time invested in dialogue and innovation. Being creative is desirable in this quadrant, but being traditional is often the norm.

The final quadrant in the matrix deals with decisions that have major impact on the people of the organization. Mergers, restructuring, philosophy changes such as moving to a team-based organization, and human resource system changes (i.e., compensation, performance management) are all decisions that belong in this quadrant. Like the major task decisions, these issues are often the very reason for bringing the team together. Decisions in this area need to be driven by constructed thinking. The issues are seldom characterized as having right answers, and involvement and acceptance are the keys to effectiveness. Rather than having an internal focus on analysis, these decisions gain value from synthesis and inclusion. Teams that deal with these decisions effectively develop a strong external focus and tolerate many variations around a general resolution. To the extent that the team can discipline itself to clarify first the type of decision it needs to make, the greater likelihood that it can focus on the relevant parts of the decision-making process. Successful teams assess and monitor this critical part of their process on a regular basis, often using outside assessors to provide both insight into the whole process and training for gaining greater decision-making capabilities.

> To the extent that the team can discipline itself to first clarify the type of decision it needs to make, the more it can focus on the relevant parts of the decision-making process.

Decision-Making Process

The normal team decision-making process revolves around throwing ideas out on the table during a team discussion period. Relying on a Darwinian effect, the team assumes that the "fittest" of the ideas will survive this process. If the team was not subject to the human liabilities of politics, persuasion, and power, this natural evolution of ideas might work. However, given the nature of organizations and teams, decision making must have some method to record and develop ideas if it is to be effective.

> Relying on a Darwinian effect, the team assumes that the "fittest" of the ideas will survive this process.

Figure 6.2 provides an example of a common decision-making process. While most teams are aware of this process, team members often do not follow it in any systematic way. The diagram shows that once the team has accepted the responsibility for the decision, it must gather information to analyze the nature of the issue. Referring back to the decision matrix at the beginning of the chapter, the team needs to monitor the time it spends on this step. The information sought must be sufficient to assure a quality decision, but gathering information cannot become an end unto itself. It often helps the team to define its purpose and set parameters on the information needed before the search begins. That way, team members know what to look for and when to stop gathering data.

Once the team has appropriate information, it can move on to generating options. If the team is deciding a major issue, gathering background information may be the most important part of the decision-making process. The more ideas and options the team can generate, the more possibilities for resolution, especially given that major issues are by definition complex and defy a "one right answer" approach. Once generated, options are developed and evaluated. The use of quality thinking and inquiring verbal behaviors enhance these discussion steps in the decision-making process. The conversation skills of both dialogue and discussion are necessary for this step to lead to enlightened decisions.

When the issue is understood and the options are articulated, the team needs to select one or more pathways to resolution. Coming to a clear and agreed upon decision

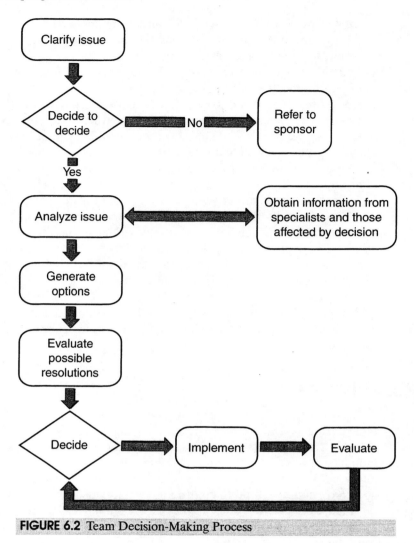

FIGURE 6.2 Team Decision-Making Process

often eludes the team. Team members frequently complain that issues are discussed and discussed but not resolved. To make progress, the team needs to make choices and move on to the next issue. Selecting the appropriate choice mechanism can help the team decide.

There are, then, three parts to the decision-making process, in particular, that teams need to manage carefully: (1) generating ideas; (2) exploring ideas; and (3) deciding on a course of action. In the following sections we will discuss each of the three parts. However, the success or failure of the decision is often in its implementation. In successful teams, the work is not done with the decision. Mutual accountability demands that the team manage the implementation of the decision and then evaluate its impact. In Part IV of the book we will discuss implementation as a part of the external focus of the team.

Generating Ideas and Options

Over the years researchers in the area of decision making have been aware that if a quality decision is to be made, quality ideas must first come from the group. In addition to generating ideas, the group needs a way to capture those ideas so that they can be explored. Without some sort of recording structure or method, most ideas will not be considered. In addition, given the political nature of the group, the ideas that are most likely to be considered are based on the position power of the suggestor. Not only does this approach discourage members of the team, it is also very detrimental to the organization because it generates few new ideas. People with high position power in the organization are generally most interested in preserving the current system that supports their position. It is unlikely that such a person will suggest an idea that will radically change the way business is done. This undermines the whole reason for the team, which is to bring in new ideas and consider new ways of doing things. Therefore, generating quality ideas is vital to the effectiveness of the team.

Brainstorming

People with high position power in the organization are generally most interested in preserving the current system that supports their position.

A common method teams use to generate ideas is brainstorming. Brainstorming is characterized by an intensive period of spawning as many ideas as possible without critique. The purpose of brainstorming is driven by the principle that if you want to end up with some good ideas, it is best to start off with many ideas. For a team to use brainstorming effectively, it must capture all the ideas, prioritize them, discuss the key ideas at length, and then decide on a course of action. To simply throw out several ideas at the beginning of the meeting is not brainstorming. In Figure 6.3 we describe three general examples of brainstorming and the advantages and disadvantages associated with each.

FIGURE 6.3 Brainstorming Techniques

Technique	Advantages	Disadvantages
Nominal Group Technique	• Controls for power • Makes efficient use of time • Establishes priorities • Can build on ideas • Preserves all ideas • Builds acceptance • Openness	• Very structured • No time for elaboration • Needs strong and objective leader • Restlessness with large group
Affinity	• Builds acceptance • Provides for small-group discussion • Shows scope and support for ideas • Controls for power • Makes efficient use of time • Preserves ideas	• Little synergism of ideas in first phase • No accommodation for second round of ideas • Requires writing skills • Requires most time
Delphi	• Does not require bringing people together • Can determine the strength of support for a given idea • Can preserve all ideas	• No synergism of ideas • People afraid of being identified • No chance for elaboration on idea • People suspicious that process has been manipulated

NOMINAL GROUP TECHNIQUE

Historically, one of the most effective methods of brainstorming has been the Nominal Group Technique (NGT). The technique, developed by Andrew Delbecq, greatly formalized the idea-generation process. The process begins with a facilitator clearly defining the problem or opportunity to be addressed. Then, in round-robin fashion, members of the group put forth ideas in short simple phrases. As is common in brainstorming, there is to be no advocacy or criticism during the idea-generation phase. The group continues to go around the table until all ideas have been expressed. All ideas are recorded and numbered on flip charts and posted around the room.

The group then spends a short time clarifying the ideas presented. The purpose here is twofold: (1) to be sure everyone understands (even if they do not agree with) the ideas listed; and (2) to eliminate duplication of ideas. Again, there is no advocacy nor criticism allowed during clarification. Once the ideas have been clarified, each member individually prioritizes the ideas recorded. This is usually done by having group members vote, in rank order, for the three to five ideas she or he thinks would be most valuable to pursue. The facilitator records each person's selections and then presents the results of the voting to the group in the form of the ideas that received the most support.

The Nominal Group Technique is very efficient. A group of 20 people can usually generate more than a hundred ideas in 15 minutes. Voting identifies those issues most acceptable to the group, and if each member in a group of 20 selects and ranks three issues, five or six will surface as the most important to pursue. Recording preserves all the ideas. Therefore, even if an issue is not substantive enough to reach the final list, it can be separately pursued as an individual "good idea."

The Nominal Group Technique also minimizes position power, because all ideas are listed in the same way, regardless of who suggested them, and the voting is done privately. Thus, a first-level employee's idea has the same opportunity for acceptance as the president's. Because of the openness of the process, the results of the voting are easily accepted by the groups as a good place to begin the exploration process.

AFFINITY

Total quality management initiatives in the early 1990s promoted a variation on the NGT called an affinity diagram. The process is similar to the NGT except that people write down their ideas and then post them on a board rather than verbally going round robin. The group then collectively sorts the ideas into general categories; that is, they group things that have an "affinity" for one another. Each category is then labeled and given to a group to decipher. The group is to combine the ideas, preserving intent and language, into a set of suggestions.

Affinity is somewhat easier to use than the NGT, though it takes more overall time. It allows everyone to generate ideas at the same time and thus reduces the restlessness that often occurs at the end of the NGT idea-generating portion when all but a few people are ready to move on. The evaluation of ideas is done in small groups, which provides for expansion and understanding. However, Affinity loses some of the power of suggestion that comes with the Nominal Group Technique. When one member of the group hears the idea of another, it may spark a new idea. In Affinity, ideas are confined initially to the mind of each member, and so the suggestions that the small teams have to work with can be fairly narrow. Both the Nominal Group Technique and Affinity gather a wealth of information from a group of people in a short period of time. The NGT is more specific in its recording and prioritizing, but Affinity gets a sense of intensity for an idea and generally has more information from which to work.

DELPHI

When a team needs to gather information from members outside the team, Delphi can be an attractive brainstorming technique. In the Delphi process, the key issue is defined and then members are polled for their suggestions. Once the suggestions are collected, the common or unusual ones are culled from the group. These suggestions then become the agenda for further discussion. Delphi allows the team to gather information from widely separated groups and to get a feeling for the support for given suggestions. The process can be repeated to gain additional information or to refine the list of suggestions. The team can also keep track of the sources of suggestions, so it would be able, for example, to separate issues and ideas associated with field offices from those associated with headquarters.

The advantages of Delphi are also its weaknesses. Like Affinity, the generation of ideas, at least in the first round, does not benefit from having heard the ideas of others. This drawback can be offset somewhat by using follow-up rounds, but some of the dynamic of the NGT is lost. The ability in Delphi to identify sources of suggestions is a tradeoff to the anonymity of both the NGT and Affinity. Depending on the sensitivity of the issue, the existence of trust in the organization, and the importance of position power, this is a more or less serious tradeoff.

Delphi, then, is most appropriately used to gain information from large, widely dispersed groups or to narrow the focus of a larger issue. All three brainstorming techniques have value to the team, and as with the decision-making process in general, the team needs to choose a technique that is well suited to the dynamics and type of decision required.

All of the brainstorming processes described above suffer from three shortcomings: originality of ideas, the size of group, and follow-through. Unless the process of brainstorming is unusually intense, the ideas generated tend to be rather ordinary. Also, the ideas presented will not necessarily give you multiple perspectives on an issue. If the group is highly homogeneous or is composed of long-term members of the organization, brainstorming will probably generate variations of ideas or practices already in use in the organization. Since brainstorming does not challenge the thinking process itself, the results tend to be shades of the familiar rather than new ideas.

One way to improve brainstorming is to require the group to go through the process several times. Edward DeBono, the corporate guru for creativity and the author of *Serious Creativity,* suggests that a group must go through at least three iterations of any brainstorming activity before it begins to generate any truly new ideas. In his approach, effective brainstorming requires the group to come up with all the ideas it can and then discard them—both literally and figuratively. Then the group starts over. By the third iteration, the group is really stretching for new responses and is most likely to be creative. As you can imagine, this type of brainstorming can be a much more time-consuming and difficult process than just a single swipe at new ideas. However, if the team is working on a major issue, the investment in time and energy is likely worthwhile.

One way to improve brainstorming is to require the group to go through the process several times.

Two final issues that determine the effectiveness of the team's use of brainstorming are group size and follow-through. It is important to take the size of the group into account when choosing a brainstorming process. If the group consists of more than 24 people, it is probably better to use Affinity than the Nominal Group Technique. As the group increases in size, it takes longer and longer for the round robin discussion to reach each person. Group members will become restless and may lose interest in the process. The larger the group, the more important it is for the facilitator to keep the process moving. With Affinity, each person works on his or her own and then gathers in small groups. There is no period of time when the individual is not immersed in the process. It is therefore easier to keep a large group involved and focused.

Brainstorming generates many ideas, some of them worth pursuing. It is important that the team identify a range of ideas to follow through on after the session and be persistent in acting on those ideas. If in the end, the process is just a list of ideas with no action having been taken, participants will become cynical and unwilling to participate in future brainstorming activities.

Reflection

Consider a team decision-making situation where you have been an active member of the process. How well did the team generate ideas? What was the impact of the process on the quality of the decision?

Idea-Generation Process Assessment		
Activity	*Application*	*Impact on Process*
Use a structured method to produce many ideas.	☐ Seldom ☐ Awkward ☐ Sometimes ☐ Inconsistent ☐ Frequent ☐ Skilled	
Assure that there is no advocacy or criticism from participants.	☐ Seldom ☐ Awkward ☐ Sometimes ☐ Inconsistent ☐ Frequent ☐ Skilled	
Capture ideas for future reference and use.	☐ Seldom ☐ Awkward ☐ Sometimes ☐ Inconsistent ☐ Frequent ☐ Skilled	
Cull out the best ideas for further discussion.	☐ Seldom ☐ Awkward ☐ Sometimes ☐ Inconsistent ☐ Frequent ☐ Skilled	
Follow up on ideas with expanded discussion/action.	☐ Seldom ☐ Awkward ☐ Sometimes ☐ Inconsistent ☐ Frequent ☐ Skilled	

Team Work

Now consider your current team.

What are the idea-generation strengths of your current team?

_____   _____

How could you better leverage these strengths? Could you increase the frequency of their use; find other situations where you could use them; and/or involve others in the process?

_____   _____
_____   _____
_____   _____

What are the idea-generation problems for your current team?

_____   _____

How could you address these problems and improve the team's skill level?

_____

_____

_____

Team Charter

Record your suggestions, ideas, and decisions in the Team Charter in the appendix of the book.

Exploring Ideas and Options

Once ideas come to the table, they must be explored and enriched. In Chapter 5 we described the process of dialogue and discussion. In the exploration phase of decision making, dialogue is the most effective conversation style. Understanding rather than judging will draw out the best insights from the team and allow people to bring forth innovative ideas.

Below we describe two important elements of effective exploration. First, we consider the need for good thinking by the team. No matter how open the group, if the thinking is not clear and disciplined, the decisions will be flawed. Next, we build on some skills begun in Chapter 5 by looking at verbal behaviors that are especially important to the exploration step in decision making.

Thinking

Thinking skills, like other human capacities, grow and develop over time. Like other skills, they are enhanced through learning and practice. Figure 6.4 is a continuum that sets forth a general evolution of thinking skills used within the organization. The least sophisticated skills are found at the left end of the scale. Received thinking skills tend to be limited and cautious, and to look for others to solve the team's problems. As such, they contribute little to team thinking, especially if the team has been called together for problem solving or opportunity pursuit. Moving up the scale, subjective thinking allows the team itself to address problems, but it tends to be very conservative and traditional in approach. Only if the team has firsthand experience with the specific issues presented will subjective thinking lend insight to the discussion. Procedural thinking is the most common form of team thinking. Teams use procedural thinking in both discussion and decision making. Unlike received and subjective thinking, procedural thinking adds greatly to the teaming process. Constructed thinking represents the most sophisticated level of team interaction. Dialogue requires constructed thinking. Teams that can blend procedural and constructed thinking have the best chance for innovative thinking and quality decisions.

Received thinking depends heavily on authority for opinions and conclusions. If the boss, the union, the manual, or for that matter the newspaper or TV says something

FIGURE 6.4 Development of Our Thinking Processes

Received	Subjective	Procedural	Constructed
• Authoritative	• Experiential	• Anwers given	• Questions raised
• Dualistic	• Owns its own authority	• Analysis made	• Synthesis sought
• Quantitative	• Goes on "gut feeling"	• Argumentative	• Exploration pursued

is so, then that ends the discussion. Therefore, received thinking tends to operate from a dualistic perspective—good/bad, right/wrong, smart/stupid—and has a great deal of trouble working well in an ambiguous environment. In received thinking, a paradox is simply not possible.

There was a time when organizations valued received thinking. People who did what they were told and did not question authority were valued; the company manual was right; competitors were evil. In today's teams, received thinking can bring discussion to a halt. It offers little capacity to deal with complexity, and risk taking is undesirable. Fear of reprisal and overvaluing tradition causes the team to fear to do anything without permission.

When a team finds its conversation studded with statements like the ones in the list below, it has fallen into received thinking and needs to challenge its discussion process:

"The boss said . . ."

"According to the report, we cannot do that."

"We have always done it that way."

"If they cannot tell us exactly what will happen, I am not buying in."

"He's wrong about that."

Subjective thinking is more developed than reactive in that it allows the team to form its own opinions. Subjective thinking fosters more willingness to consider new approaches. The drawback in subjective thinking is that opinions and conclusions tend to be based only on emotion. When the team relies on subjective thinking, it does not seek out facts and does not value other points of view. These teams are likely to ignore policies that they think are "stupid" or information deemed "irrelevant" in favor of the experience of team members. It is not easy for teams engaged in subjective thinking to imagine; if a team member has not seen something work, it simply will not work.

Teams are likely to slip into subjective thinking when issues become complex and information hard to understand. Frustrated by facts and figures, the conversation reverts to statements like:

"I just know it will work."

"Maybe they are right, but I am not going along."

"I have never seen it work before."

"That's what the manual says, but I know better."

"If you haven't been here 20 years, you just can't understand."

The "gut feeling" that comes from subjective thinking can be valuable to the decision process. However, it cannot be confused with fact. Unlike received thinking, subjective thinking can be brought forward along the thinking continuum as part of developing more complex thinking skills.

PROCEDURAL THINKING

Procedural thinking is where most teams operate. Most managerial training and administrative systems are based on procedural thinking. The value of procedural thinking is in its method. Procedural thinking breaks things apart for analysis and is reliant on information. It can deal with complexity and create strategy. The shortcoming of procedural thinking lies in its search for "the" answer, its dependence on objectivity, and its overuse of critique. Procedural thinking is useful for dealing with bounded problems for which there are right answers (numbers-based problems) and for assessing past situations. It is necessary for choosing options, candidates, and proposals. It is not useful for innovation, negotiation, or for solving problems for which there are no "right" answers (i.e., customer satisfaction).

Teams know they are engaged in procedural thinking when they hear statements such as:

"Let's vote."

"We need to control . . ."

"What's wrong with this approach is . . ."

"There are 3 ways we could solve this."

"Let's divide it up."

"They all agreed, so it must be the right thing to do."

Procedural thinking is best suited for the choosing part of the decision-making process. Constructed thinking is much more valuable for the exploration step.

CONSTRUCTED THINKING

Constructed thinking requires the use of both subjective and procedural thinking plus an ability to imagine and a willingness to consider multiple pathways for resolution. Constructed thinking focuses more on understanding than knowing; on asking the right questions rather than having the right answers. When the team engages in constructed thinking, it is willing and able to blend intuitive and factual information and to value both subjective and objective information. Both experience and abstract information have a place in deciding, and outside information is seen as an asset, not a challenge. Since the team recognizes that there is more than one way to do things, suggestions from others do not result in defensiveness. Two of the most useful aspects of constructed thinking are its ability to deal with ambiguity and its willingness to challenge the status quo. Not fearing ambiguity allows the team to embrace change. Rather than frustrating the team, new ideas and information invigorate it. Constructed thinking encourages the team to challenge its mindsets; to look at things differently; and to value multiple perspectives.

A team knows it is engaging in constructed thinking when it hears:

"No one has ever tried this before."

"How will this affect others?"

"What other ways could we do it?"

"These numbers support the feeling I have that . . ."

"What if they didn't react that way?"

"What will the whole thing look like?"

"These changes offer us many opportunities."

Constructed thinking does not encourage all team members to agree. In fact, differences in opinion are valued. Complex problems do not lend themselves to single solutions. Differences in opinion should lead to different methods for addressing specific issues. With the demands for speed in today's work environment, there is no time for proceeding in a sequential manner. Yet many decision-making practices demand just that. The team agrees on one path of action and pursues that until all team members are convinced that it is not working or has become obsolete, and only then does the team look for another way. Constructed thinking encourages the use of multiple pathways for action. If we work on ideas in parallel, not only have we increased our likelihood of finding methods that work, but we have made synergy possible. Doing things in sequence does not allow for synergy, because there is no interaction between activities. The best one can hope for is a good memory so that you do not repeat the same mistakes. Multiple paths for action allow team members to learn from each other and to come together or continue on their separate ways depending on the need.

Constructed thinking is not "better" than procedural thinking; it is simply different. Because team members tend to be much more familiar with and skilled in procedural thinking, the team uses it for everything. Successful teams learn the skills of constructed thinking and use them when appropriate and especially in the exploration activities of the team. Procedural and constructed thinking support the discussion and dialogue dimensions of conversation respectively as discussed in Chapter 5. Figure 6.5 shows the movement from procedural to constructed thinking.

CHALLENGE ASSUMPTIONS

Another useful way to improve team thinking is through a process that challenges the current assumptions of the group. A team conversation with this focus begins by clarifying the assumptions that the group holds about the problem or issue presented. Once those assumptions are listed, the group is asked to challenge or reverse them and then to use these new assumptions as the basis for brainstorming activity. An example will help clarify this process.

Imagine yourself as the city manager for a small city. You are under increasing pressure to provide more services to your citizens; to provide them in a faster time frame; and at the same time to contain costs. You have brought together a cross-functional process improvement team to find ways to improve the way the administrative services of the city operate.

FIGURE 6.5 Thinking Styles for Effective Decision Making

Procedural Thinking		Constructed Thinking
Bounded issues	➡	Complex issues
Answers	➡	Questions
Analysis	➡	Synthesis
Argue; defend	➡	Explore
Relies on method	➡	Challenges assumptions
Vertical; sequential	➡	Lateral; parallel
Reduce; separate	➡	Expand; holistic
Judgmental	➡	Accepting
Controlling	➡	Self-organizing
Objective; impersonal	➡	Intuitive and factual
Multiple realities	➡	Multiple perspectives
Knowing; one right answer	➡	Understanding; no absolute truth

This is a very typical quality-management team scenario. Under normal discussion processes, the team would begin to come up with ways to be more efficient. The team would likely talk about how to improve the process of issuing licenses, holding hearings, dealing with complaints, and so forth. The focus would be on how we can better do what we do. This is a laudable task but will probably not result in any truly new ideas.

Now, if the group first begins by challenging assumptions, the course the team follows could be much different. For example, the process improvement team described above might come up with the following assumptions:

- You need to have a license to do business with the city.
- People need to come to this office to get licenses.
- The city needs to issue the licenses.
- Our customers are not smart enough to understand the licensing process.
- The office is open from 8 to 5, Monday through Friday.
- Exception hearings must be held in our hearings rooms.

Take the first assumption. If the team challenges this assumption, they would say that you do not need a license to do business with the city. The team could then discuss what would happen if business licenses were eliminated and how the impact would be different for different types of licenses. The results might be that the team recommends that several licensing processes simply be abolished. Under the old brainstorming method the team would likely consider ways to do the licensing process faster rather than eliminate it altogether.

As the team challenges its current assumptions, it begins to look for new ways to do things that are outside those assumptions. Just because the team challenges an assumption does not mean that it cannot, in the end, validate that assumption. However, in the exploration part of decision making, it is important for the team to be able to "turn things upside down" and explore options outside the normal mindset of the team.

How the team explores ideas, therefore, has a great impact on the effectiveness of its decision making. Unless teams change the way they traditionally make decisions, they will not be able to reap the benefit of the new thinking and new ideas that organizations expect from teams.

Successful teams focus on skill development within the decision-making process. Thinking is a discipline that is gaining recognition as a critical part of the team and of the decision-making process. Teams that include thinking skills as part of their development and evaluation process are well on their way to enhancing their decision-making competencies.

Reflection

Think about a team where you have been an active participant. How well did the team think?

Team Work

Consider your current team.

What are your team's shortcomings when it comes to thinking skills?

_____

_____

_____

Level of Thinking	Frequency of Use	Example and Impact on Team
Received Thinking	☐ Seldom ☐ Sometimes ☐ Frequent	Example: Impact:
Subjective Thinking	☐ Seldom ☐ Sometimes ☐ Frequent	Example: Impact:
Procedural Thinking	☐ Seldom ☐ Sometimes ☐ Frequent	Example: Impact:
Constructed Thinking	☐ Seldom ☐ Sometimes ☐ Frequent	Example: Impact:

How do these shortcomings impact the team?

_____

_____

_____

What could you do to improve the thinking skills within the team?

_____

_____

_____

Team Charter

Record your suggestions, ideas, and decisions in the Team Charter in the appendix of the book.

Verbal Behaviors

To take advantage of methods like dialogue and to improve its way of thinking, the team must also change its language. In Chapter 5 we considered the verbal skills that influenced the quality of participation among team members. In this section we will look at the verbal behaviors that impact decision making. The language the team uses greatly influences the quality of ideas generated and the willingness of team members to share those ideas. There are five interactive behaviors that impact the team's ability to engage in effective decision making:

- proposing
- building
- clarification
- ridicule
- arguing

Propose: Suggest a course of action

Meetings are often characterized by lots of talk and little action. The primary reason for this is that people prefer to share their opinions more than they like to take the risk of making suggestions. As a result, opinions abound but without direction. In order for discussion to move the group forward, team members must suggest alternatives for action. Effective teams continually move from general talk to recommended action. Proposing is the verbal behavior that causes this shift. In the spirit of dialogue, these recommendations need to be enriched and preserved for use when the team moves to a final decision.

Proposing is a suggestion for a course of action. Proposals can come in the form of either a statement or a question. "Let's change the specifications to require follow-up service" is a proposal statement. "Should we recommend the downtown convention center to the executive committee?" is a question-based proposal. They both suggest action. However, the question-based proposal is softer and encourages continuing discussion. Team members who have strong position power relative to the rest of the group should consider using question-based proposals. Team members who are quiet or who are trying to establish their role in the team might do better to use the stronger proposal statement.

Another type of proposal that is very helpful to the team is a process proposal. This type of proposal suggests process action. Process proposals would include suggestions such as:

> "Let's spend the first half of the meeting just generating ideas and then after a break we can come back and make our decision."

> "Let's gather information from our key customers before we make the final decision."

Process proposals suggest "how" the team should accomplish something, not the specifics of "what" it should do. Many people are reluctant to discuss substantive issues until they understand the process rules of the game.

Process proposals are particularly important because they can get a reluctant team started or a stuck team moving. To get the team moving, a team member might propose:

> "Let's just go around the table and get an initial reaction to the new legislation."

> "Let's use an Affinity process before we begin our discussion so we get all the problems out on the table."

To get a team through a discussion log jam, a team member might suggest:

> "We have been going in circles on this for over an hour. Let's assign it to a subcommittee for recommended action."

> "Let's put the cost issue aside for awhile and discuss desired outcomes."

Verbal behaviors that propose action keep the team moving. Without proposals, both the process and substantive kind, the team treads water and often loses its energy. If the team discussion seems to be stagnant and repetitive, team members need to see how many suggestions for action have been made recently. Such a search will probably reveal that the team has just been giving information and opinions and not making proposals. The team can then focus on recommended actions and make progress.

Building: Expanding and developing the proposal of another

Another interaction behavior that helps the team with discussion is building. Building refers to the process of expanding and enriching a proposal made by another.

Ideas are seldom presented in complete form. They are frequently just snippets of information, and in their initial form they often seem unworkable. The verbal behavior of building allows the team to add to initial ideas to create a complete recommendation or plan:

> "If we replace the old computers we could then donate them to the 'adopt a school' program we are supporting."

> "In addition to presentations at the sales conference we could bring some prototypes to demonstrate the improvements we expect in the new product line."

Both are building statements. They take the original idea of another and expand on it.

Another powerful dimension of the verbal behavior of building is its ability to let a team member change direction without rejecting the ideas of others. As emphasized before, a key condition for dialogue is nonjudgment. Say that during the exploration part of decision making, team members reject ideas they have prematurely moved to the deciding phase of the decision-making process. Instead of focusing on rejection, team members can refocus the discussion and preserve the option. For example, a team member might say:

> "I agree that we need to provide these inspections for our customers, but I think we should open several substations around the city rather than require people to come to the main office."

> "We should be able to manage the project in the time frame you suggest, but what if we brought in some contract people just to be sure?"

Building is one of the most important verbal behaviors team members can master. It provides for well-thought-out proposals for action, a feeling among team members that each has been listened to, and a way to disagree without being disagreeable. This is a huge return for an investment in a single verbal behavior. The drawback is that building is hard to do. First, it requires that the team member listen carefully to the ideas expressed by others. Listening requires attention and a focus on the speaker rather than on oneself.

The second requirement for the team to develop the verbal behavior of building is that team members forego their reliance on debate. Debate encourages arguing and counterproposals, and stresses using one's own idea rather than considering the other person's idea. Building encourages the integration of several concepts to develop a complete idea. Building is an essential skill for constructed thinking.

Clarify: Ask questions to assure that the idea is clearly understood by the entire team

Communication is an imprecise art. The differences in meaning between what the sender intends and what the receiver understands are often vast. Disagreements in decision making are as often based on misunderstanding as on true differences in opinion. If the team is going to understand issues and ideas, it must learn to ask clarifying questions regularly. Clarifying questions include:

> "Tell me again how this will work."

> "Did you say the proposal would be ready by the end of the week?"

> "Can you give me an example so I can understand?"

Occasionally, a team member will feel that she or he could benefit from a misunderstanding. For example, the team is about to agree to a course of action but does not understand all of the implications from such an action. If the team member is likely to benefit from the action, it is hard for that person to raise the clarifying questions to be sure that the team understands exactly what it is getting into. However, if the team decides on the basis of misinformation, the results are seldom positive. The best case response is that when the team gets correct information, it will need to go back and discuss and decide the issue again. Those who supported the initial decision may be reluctant to go through the process again. The worst-case response is that the team members who should have sought clarification are seen as deceptive, and team trust is damaged.

To be effective, the team needs to operate from good, clear information and ideas. Because misunderstanding is so easy in a group of 8 to 12 people who all filter information according to their own perspectives, the team needs to consciously use clarifying verbal behaviors to keep misunderstanding from being the norm.

Ridicule: Criticism focused on the presenter

Teams often tie the value of an idea to the person who presents it. Support or criticism of the idea then becomes personal rather than based on the idea itself. The result is that the proposer becomes defensive if the idea is criticized and indebted if the idea is supported. Either way, it becomes difficult to accept or amend the idea. Ridicule is a verbal behavior that focuses criticism on the proposer of the idea rather than on the idea itself. The use of ridicule is a very common problem in team decision making, and team members must make a special effort to control this behavior. One indicator that the team discussion has slipped into ridicule is if you hear people using the word "you." When the word "you" is the focus, then the idea has lost focus. For example, if a team member responds to an idea about a way to keep costs down with

"You always have to think of the bottom line,"

the discussion has shifted away from costs and on to the person.

Another indicator that the discussion has shifted to the personal is the use of judgment words. An example would be a team-member response to a suggestion that the team run its recommendation past the other divisions such as:

"You are always so political. I don't care if the other divisions don't like this. It is the right thing to do."

Phrases like "you are always so political" cast judgment on the person rather than the idea being discussed. Judgment words are fighting words. The person is likely to take umbrage with the remark and get defensive and perhaps hostile. The result is that the team discussion is damaged and the issue is lost.

It is very difficult for the team to move focus back to the issue once a personal attribution has been made. People can differ on issues and still maintain respect and trust. Once the focus is personal, however, both are often lost. Teams can minimize the use of ridicule in team discussion through the use of ground rules designed to emphasize how to make things work rather than what is wrong with an idea. The team can also develop good questioning skills. Drawing out information on the idea and allowing it to ripen will help the group determine its value and avoid personal attacks.

Argue: Challenge another's position; lecture

As discussed earlier, the real value gained from working with teams is bringing multiple perspectives together to address an issue. In order to realize that value, the team must accept those differing ideas of team members. While the team usually agrees that this is desirable, and even makes ground rules to reinforce the desire for multiple perspectives, the verbal behavior of arguing often undoes that intent.

Arguing is challenging and cutting off the ideas and suggestions of another. It is usually characterized by quick reaction to an initial statement. Typical arguing behaviors include:

"That will not work because . . ."

"You are wrong about . . ."

"I think two weeks is enough."

In our discussion on conversation in Chapter 5, we talked about the pervasiveness of debate as a model for our verbal interactions. Arguing behaviors are very much a part of the debate process, and their primary intent is to cut off discussion of the other person's ideas.

Within the decision-making process, arguing interferes with the team's ability to explore and fully develop alternatives. Arguing also makes it very difficult for the team to consider multiple options because argument is fundamentally driven by a concept of a right-and-wrong approach. One of the ways that successful teams minimize arguing is by separating the options-generating part of decision making from the deciding part. This separation encourages nonjudgment and allows the team to enforce brainstorming rules. Even in the deciding part of the process, the successful team tries to encourage questioning behaviors to clarify options rather than arguing behaviors that cut off disclosure.

As in participation, it does matter what and how you say things in decision making. Words and tone are not neutral. They greatly influence the climate of team interaction and the quality of results. Talking is so natural to people that they often forget to monitor its effectiveness. Successful teams work to develop sophisticated, verbal behaviors and to monitor the quality of team conversation on a regular basis.

Reflection

Reflect on team meetings you have attended in the past, and evaluate how effectively team members used verbal behaviors.

Team being assessed: _____

Verbal Behavior	Frequency of Use			Impact on Team
	Seldom	Sometimes	Often	
Propose				
Build				
Clarify				
Ridicule				
Argue				

Team Work

Now, consider your current team.

What positive verbal behaviors are absent from your current team meetings?

_____   _____
_____   _____

How would adding these behaviors help the team?_____
_____
_____

What negative verbal behaviors do you see your team using? _____
_____
_____

How might you minimize the use of these behaviors?_____
_____

Team Charter

Record your suggestions, ideas, and decisions in the Team Charter in the appendix of the book.

Deciding on Action

Once the team has discussed options thoroughly, and understanding of context and content is clear, it is time to make a choice. Choice does not mean a focus on one and only one answer, but it invariably means narrowing the paths to follow.

The team can employ a variety of methods for making choices that go from a general sense of agreement to a mathematically based prioritizing process. Depending on the maturity and trust level of the team and on the complexity of the task, the team may choose from one or a combination of methods.

Figure 6.6 describes methods that fall at different points along the choice continuum. Justified decision making represents a process that is driven by the weight of fact and logic. By their nature, these decisions are largely procedural, relying as they do on structure and calculation to bring forth a "correct" decision. The process of Rational Decision Making developed by Kepner and Tregoe in the 1960s is perhaps the best articulated and most widely used of the justified decision-making methods, but other techniques such as decision trees are a common part of a logic-based decision-making process.

At the other end of the choice continuum is consensus, an agreement-based choice process. That it is agreement-based does not mean that consensus is void of logic. However, in consensus, it is the drive to agreement that validates the logic. That is, if we all agree, then this option must be the right course of action. Compare this belief with the one that drives justified decision making: If we can justify a course of action through evidence and logic, it follows that everyone will agree. It is just logical!

In the middle of the continuum is a process that draws from both ends of the continuum. Teams need to use facts to clarify and understand the complexity of an issue.

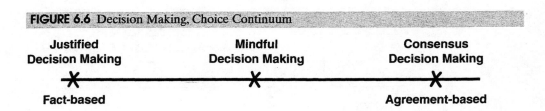

FIGURE 6.6 Decision Making, Choice Continuum

Justified Decision Making	Mindful Decision Making	Consensus Decision Making
X	X	X
Fact-based		Agreement-based

Without good information, team thinking is incomplete. The team must also deal with member feelings and the emotional issue of commitment to the decision. The team does not need to reach consensus, but it does need a level of agreement. Mindful decision making, the midpoint on the continuum, draws from information and emotion to attain the minimal amount of agreement that will allow for differences but still engender commitment to an overall direction.

JUSTIFIED DECISION MAKING

Justified decision making attempts to take emotion and bias out of decision making, or at least to bring it to a manageable level. This approach asks team members first to identify the criteria for making a good decision. These might be price, features, schedule, and so forth. Once the criteria are set, each alternative can be objectively weighed against the criteria. The option that receives the highest score is the first choice.

A common example for justified decision making is buying a car. The criteria might include the price of the car, the standard equipment included, the repair record for that make and model car, expected miles per gallon, availability of financing, and so forth. The person using a justified decision-making model first has to decide which of the criteria represent requirements and which represent desirables. For our example, let's say the most the person can afford to pay for a car is $20,000. Therefore, a price of $20,000 or less is a requirement, and any car that is presented as an alternative MUST satisfy this criterion to receive further consideration. Having a radio, air conditioning, or antilock brakes are likely desirables, and each is rated in terms of importance to the person buying the car. Once requirements are identified and desirables are ranked, the person looks at car choices. Each model of car considered receives a numerical rating (from 1 to 10) based on the degree to which it satisfies the person's desires. The model is not considered if it does not meet the requirements—in this case a price of less than $20,000. Figure 6.7 depicts the justified decision-making process for buying a car as described above.

FIGURE 6.7 Justified Decision Making: Choosing a Car

REQUIREMENTS: Price less than $20,000

DESIRABLES:

	Weight
Air conditioning	7
CD player	5
ABS brakes	2
Good repair record	8
Good gas mileage	6

Alternatives	*Air*	*CD*	*ABS*	*Repair*	*Gas*	*Total*
Car 1	6 ×7	2 ×5	6 ×2	5 ×8	7 ×6	146
Car 2	6 ×7	10 ×5	10 ×2	8 ×8	8 ×6	224
Car 3	2 ×7	5 ×5	0 ×2	5 ×8	7 ×6	121
Car 4	10 ×7	8 ×5	10 ×2	9 ×8	6 ×6	238

CHOICE: Car 4

While this process may seem contrived, justified decision making is the basis of many decisions made in business. Sometimes the use of justified decision making is very clear, as when a company requests proposals for a project. Proposal evaluators often use strict justified decision-making approaches to evaluate bids. In other instances, the method is more oblique, but the fundamental assumptions of justified decision making still prevail; that is, each alternative is given a value, and the alternative with the highest value is chosen.

Sometimes the value is numeric and clearly stated, as when a company calculates expected return from a new product or selects a new piece of equipment. Sometimes the value is more emotional, as when an alternative is chosen on the basis of the sponsor's personal ability to persuade or as in the selection process used to bring new people into the organization. Whichever the type of calculation, the result is the same. All alternatives are compared, and a single "best" choice is made based on the weight of the evidence.

Teams that use justified decision making usually find it quite efficient, if not always effective. Some criteria are hard to articulate, and team members often withhold their true preferences for fear of ridicule from the rest of the group. For example, drawing on the example of choosing a car, Car 4, which received the most points, turns out to be a conservative four-door sedan. The car satisfies the price constraint, gets good gas mileage, has a good repair record and the desired equipment. While this might be a "right" and practical decision, it can leave the buyer disappointed. Perhaps the buyer wanted a car with some style that would impress his or her friends. It may not seem logical or practical to include this criteria in the decision-making matrix. The more emotional issues of "pizzazz" and status can easily be left out of the justified decision-making process, resulting in practical but common decisions. Thus, decisions made with this method seldom engender outright rebellion, because the process is outwardly unbiased, but indifference is a common response. The process is logical, the decision is logical, and the commitment is logical. Unfortunately, logical commitment often does not generate much energy and enthusiasm.

Justified decision making can provide a useful decision-making process to teams, and it is particularly valuable for new teams or teams faced with very complex issues, because it provides a step-by-step way to proceed toward decision making. Justified decision making is commonly used for making major task decisions. The weakness of justified decision making lies in its illusion of and dependence on objectivity. If the team gets caught up in the mechanics of the process and fails to allow for the feelings of team members, the decision making becomes hollow.

CONSENSUS

A more emotional and less structured approach to decision making is consensus. When a team uses consensus as its guide for decision making, everyone must agree and fully accept the decision of the team. There is an expectation in consensus that the level of acceptance be both equal and enthusiastic.

However, anyone who has ever been involved in team decision making knows how difficult it is for every member of the team to agree to a decision with equal commitment. The energy and time needed for every member to reach consensus is enormous. And there is always the possibility that one or more persons simply will not or cannot go along. The decision-making process then comes to a halt and often deteriorates into finger pointing and argument.

The biggest problem with consensus, however, is its assumption that agreement indicates a quality decision. That is, we have confidence in the decision because we all agree. There is no real basis for such a conclusion. Agreement has little to do with the quality of the decision we are making. In fact, agreement is probably a more common indicator of poor quality than disagreement would be. An overemphasis on consensus can lead to groupthink, a group behavior that favors agreement over quality. We will discuss groupthink in Chapter 12 on renewal in Part IV of the book.

Team members need to determine the value of consensus for a decision before they begin discussion. The more the decision represents a core value or principle, the more consensus is important. In these situations, the team needs to be of common mind, and it is worthwhile for the team to take the time to reach a consensus level of agreement.

MINDFUL DECISION MAKING

Teams in today's organizations will usually be most effective if they choose a decision-making process between the two ends of the continuum (see Figure 6.6). Reflecting on the various demands placed on teams, the choice process needs to be more considered than prescribed; that is, as the team reaches the choice phase of the decision-making process, it needs to consciously define the choice method it will use.

If the choice is a bounded one, the team will move toward a justified decision-making method. Bounded decisions are characterized by clear-cut parameters (boundaries) and a relatively narrow definition for a right answer. Team decisions that fall into this category might include a site for a new building, choice of a vendor to provide a product, or choice of a major piece of equipment. For these decisions the emphasis is primarily technical. The decisions are major and the implications may be great, but they tend to be technical in nature.

When the team decision is primarily concerned with commitment, the choice process needs to focus on consensus. Defining a shared vision for the organization, changes in organizational structure, and customer satisfaction initiatives are examples of this type of decision making.

Reflection

Consider a team decision-making situation where you have been an active member of the process. How well did they differentiate and use action-deciding processes? What was the impact of the process on the quality of the decision?

Team Work

Now consider your current team.

What are the choice process strengths of your current team?

_____   _____

How could you better leverage these strengths? In other words, how could you clarify their use and monitor their effectiveness?

_____
_____
_____

What are the choice problems for your current team?

_____   _____

How could you address these problems and improve the team's skill level?

_____
_____
_____

Idea-Generation Process Assessment				
Activity	*Application*		*Impact on Process*	
Use a justified decision-making process.	☐ Seldom ☐ Sometimes ☐ Frequent	☐ Awkward ☐ Inconsistent ☐ Skilled		
Include emotional issues within the justified decision-making process.	☐ Seldom ☐ Sometimes ☐ Frequent	☐ Awkward ☐ Inconsistent ☐ Skilled		
Identify when a consensus level of agreement was appropriate.	☐ Seldom ☐ Sometimes ☐ Frequent	☐ Awkward ☐ Inconsistent ☐ Skilled		
Use dialogue to develop consensus.	☐ Seldom ☐ Sometimes ☐ Frequent	☐ Awkward ☐ Inconsistent ☐ Skilled		
Identify the need to include both logic and agreement in process.	☐ Seldom ☐ Sometimes ☐ Frequent	☐ Awkward ☐ Inconsistent ☐ Skilled		
Able to include facts, feelings, and tolerate a level of disagreement.	☐ Seldom ☐ Sometimes ☐ Frequent	☐ Awkward ☐ Inconsistent ☐ Skilled		

Team Charter

Record your suggestions, ideas, and decisions in the Team Charter in the appendix of the book.

Making decisions, then, is the primary work of the team. To do it well, the team needs to pay attention to how it generates ideas, discusses options, and comes to a decision. Effective teams are aware of the process alternatives available to them at each stage of decision making and consciously choose approaches appropriate to the decision needed.

Conclusion

Developing a team process maximizes efficiency. There are three phases an efficient team must go through: formation, development, and renewal. These phases are evolutionary in progress and require team commitment and communication to pass the breakpoints between the phases. The formation phase deals with more than just the make-up of the team. It includes adjustment within the team, which is where team ground rules, roles, and responsibilities are solidified. The development phase includes cohesion and reinforcement, which enables teams to focus on tasks. Development deals with how teams perceive themselves and their tasks. The renewal phase encompasses learning and transformation, and for the teams that work through the breakpoints, serves as a reward for improved formation and development. Key learnings from previous processes are evaluated and applied to restructuring for the next level of team work.

End of Section Activities

Discussion Questions

1. Discuss the key process ground rules for meeting management.
2. Explain ways that clear work expectations with team members can be communicated.
3. Discuss the different levels of communication in a group.
4. List the key participation problems that teams face. How can they be resolved by the team?
5. Define the various types of decisions that teams make.
6. List examples of verbal behaviors that improve group decision making.

Application: Critical Incident

You are a project manager responsible for developing a satellite office in South America. There have been thefts during the transportation of capital equipment to the new site. You must discuss this in your team meeting, but widespread discussion could impact on the timeframe for operationalizing the new site. How can you ensure that team members will use the confidential information to improve, rather than jeopardize, future transportations?

Reinforcement: Exercises

OBSERVATION

Using the Ground Rules Process Assessment in Chapter 4, interview 5 members representing different teams and see how many of them have the ground rules in place. Include comments on the effectiveness of the ground rules if the teams have them in place, and the impact of having no ground rules.

1. Ground rules in place: Covert _____ Overt _____
2. Overall value of each ground rule
3. Topics with no ground rules and their impact

OBSERVATION

Using the Team Decision-Making Matrix in Chapter 6, interview a team member by asking questions that will provide answers to the following:

1. What quadrant of Impact and Focus was the decision and why? _____

_____

2. Based on the description of the process, were all steps listed on the matrix followed? If not, which steps were omitted? _____

_____

3. What was the outcome of the team decision? ___

_____

PART II

Creating a Team Culture

Learning from this section:

■ To understand the role culture plays in creating an effective team.

■ To be able to identify the elements that create an effective team culture.

■ To be able to measure the cultural aspect of teams.

■ To understand how to change culture to make the team more effective.

Other things I want to learn about creating a team culture:

■

■

Culture is a key to external adaptation and to internal integration, two main ingredients for team success.

The first two parts of the team puzzle focused on pieces that were technical in nature and, therefore, quite concrete to deal with. The next two parts, culture and politics, move away from the technical and deal with the more ambiguous aspects of team effectiveness.

The elements of effective teamwork described in this chapter are more difficult to define and measure, but that does not mean that they are less real, or that they have less impact on the team simply because we have to look carefully to uncover them. Often, when people describe effective teams, they talk about an espirit de corps, a relationship among team members that goes beyond simply getting a project done. That "something special" is a strong team culture. The elements that make each team unique come together to create a culture that must be understood and managed if the team is to achieve high performance.

Importance of Culture

Culture defines "how the team gets things done" and refers to the attitudes, assumptions, interactions, and methods the team uses. Every team has a culture, though not every team sets out to create its own culture. Each member of a team brings his or her own experiences and beliefs to the table. These individual dimensions need to be blended to create the culture of the team. If the issues of culture are not specifically addressed by the team, there are liable to be many inconsistencies among team members. This will likely lead to personal conflict as the team progresses and team members make assumptions about what they need to do and how they need to act relative to team activities and assignments.

Some of the elements of team culture need to be addressed early on in the life of the team. This is especially true of values that form the foundation for culture. Other aspects of culture, which are actually the demonstration and reinforcement of cultural values (i.e., rituals), are tied to given team events and are thus more spontaneous. It is important that the team consciously and continually define and shape its culture. Culture is a key to external adaptation and to internal integration, two main ingredients for team success. By defining and agreeing how to handle important issues, the team creates an effective organizational unit (Czamiawski-Joerges, 1992).

Values

Learning from this chapter:

- Define the meaning of team commitment to its purpose.

- Develop strategies to hold team mutually accountable for results.

- Identify tools to build trust within a team.

- Identify indicators of a positive culture.

- Recognize actions necessary to develop a supportive culture.

Other things I want to learn about team values:

-
-

Values are beliefs about what is good or bad, important or not important. Values lead to beliefs, and those specify behavior. To work well together, the team must share some basic values.

Culture defines "how the team gets things done" and refers to the attitudes, assumptions, interactions, and methods the team uses.

Team values tend to center around the espirit de corps of the team. Values are more subtle and more enduring than team ground rules. They determine the performance ethic of the team. Strong performance values allow the team to take the risks associated with conflict, trust, interdependence, and hard work. Following are some of the key performance values for a team to address.

Commitment

Commitment speaks to reaching agreement to engage in the tasks the team is undertaking. Team members join the team with different levels of interest and motivation. Some members are volunteers who view the team's work as consistent with what they view as important to themselves and the organization. Other members are volunteered. They join the team at the request of someone else. Members who have been volunteered tend to have less initial interest in the team.

In discussing teams, you often hear complaints about people coming to team meetings with different agendas. The complaint suggests that bringing a personal agenda to a meeting is a wrong thing to do. Actually, it is a very natural thing to do. Each member comes with an agenda of what she or he thinks the team should do and what his/her relationship will be with the team. Team members need to discuss these differing agendas, not in a judgmental way, but as a means to deciding how the team should operate. Assigning team members different roles and responsibilities can address the differing levels of commitment. Although core members of the team must, over time, do substantively equal amounts of work, that does not mean that all members must contribute in the same way or at a constant level. External pressures often cause commitment to ebb and flow. As long as overall expectations are defined and adhered to, the team can tolerate and even benefit from different levels of member input.

> **Commitment in the team comes in two forms: Commitment to task achievement and commitment to the other team members.**

An example of a common situation that impacts commitment in the business community is tax season. Accountants who serve on advisory boards or community action teams are usually clear to state their participation constraints. They sign up for activities that do not conflict with tax season and make sure team members know they are committed to the team's purpose but will not be heavily involved for a specific time of the year. Once the team understands the agendas and obligations of fellow team members, they are usually able to arrange the team's work so that all can equitably participate.

Commitment in the team comes in two forms. Commitment to task achievement and commitment to the other team members. The team must come to agreement on what is an acceptable level of commitment to the team and what behaviors demonstrate that commitment. Volunteering to do work outside of the team meetings might be an indication of commitment to the task. Meeting quality expectations and deadlines would be another.

> **Commitment speaks to reaching agreement to engage in the tasks the team is undertaking.**

Willingness to help a teammate or giving credit to a teammate for an accomplishment would be examples of behaviors consistent with commitment to the team. If the team is to achieve its potential, commitment to both task and team must be part of the culture of the team.

Teams often address commitment issues with ground rules on attendance and dependability. But this delineation is not enough. Unless the ground rules are the conclusion of a deeper discussion on commitment, they will simply be rules and will lack the very commitment they were meant to establish in the first place. For example, when teams are formed, members often set ground rules for their work together. Usually team members set a ground rule around coming to meetings prepared. However, the team seldom discusses how being prepared will help the team; what being prepared actually means; and, perhaps most important, whether everyone is really willing to come to each meeting well prepared. Unless these issues are honestly and thoroughly discussed, the team will have troubles ahead. The team members who take the ground rule seriously and come to meetings prepared will be resentful of those who do not come prepared. Those unprepared often comment that they thought the ground rules were just an opening discussion to get acquainted and did not take them very seriously. Some of those team members labeled "unprepared" will be offended and say that they thought they were prepared. "Being prepared" has different meanings for different people. Thus, teams and team members need to clearly define what commitment means to them.

Reflection

COMMITMENT ISSUES

Think about a time when you were a member of a team. Did you have a clear idea of what the commitment level of the team members was? Did you spend time addressing the following commitment questions?

- What amount of time are we willing to spend on team activities?
- How much time are we willing to spend outside of meeting time?
- Where does the team's project fall in relationship to other priorities?
- How is the team project tied to the performance objectives for each team member?
- What support are you going to receive from those higher in the organization?
- What resources are you going to receive?

Team Work

With a current team, discuss the preceding questions and issues and come to agreement on what is an acceptable level of commitment for your team.

Team Charter

Your team decisions can be recorded in the team charter in the appendix at the end of the book.

Accountability

Closely tied to the team's sense of commitment is the degree to which it holds itself accountable for the results of the team. In Chapter 2 the team identified its purpose. Accountability to that purpose depends on the team's taking responsibility for getting the task done.

The overall organizational culture will influence the underlying sense of team accountability. For example, if the organization believes strongly in individual accountability, the team will need to define how individual work will lead to team success. If the organization emphasizes chain of command, the team must be sure to define its accountability relationship with the next level of management. If the organization has a weak performance culture, the team will be in danger of focusing more on just meeting rather than on achieving results. Therefore, in addition to setting goals, the team must decide how to be mutually responsible for outcomes.

Accountability is a primary concern for the organizations who use teams. Mutual accountability is not an easy concept to understand or accept in US organizations. In the US, individual ingenuity and creativity are at the core of performance. Accordingly, the key to motivation is thought to reside within the individual employee. Our organizational reward systems are a clear indication of such orientation. Thus, there is a certain uneasiness about holding a team responsible for outcomes. Common organizational expressions like "a camel is a horse designed by a team" do not add to our confidence in team accountability.

Misgivings about team effectiveness and mutual accountability are more organizational folklore than reality. Organizational history is replete with stories of teams who have chosen to be accountable: start-up teams like NASA and Saturn; turn-around teams at Xerox, Harley-Davidson, and Hanover Insurance; and ongoing teams at Johnsonville Sausage, Motorola, and 3M. Teams can clearly be mutually accountable for results if the team makes that expectation part of its culture.

The enemies of accountability are indifference and blame.

Examples of what different levels of teams might hold themselves accountable for include:

Management Teams
- overall unit performance
- culture change
- improved image
- employee morale

Task Teams	• acceptance of team ideas by others
	• meeting deadlines
	• innovative ideas
Work Teams	• team relationships
	• quality/quantity expectations
	• customer satisfaction

If team members individually hold themselves accountable for the team's OVERALL purpose and define each individual's roles and responsibilities from a holistic view of that purpose, the team will achieve mutual accountability. That is, the team cannot accomplish its purpose unless each member views his or her own actions as part of an overall responsibility. It is not enough to get your own task done. You must be concerned about all tasks getting done. With each person contributing, the team develops a cadence and synergism and is able to accomplish more than just a summation of individual effort. This is team accountability—members being mutually responsible for the team's actions.

The enemies of accountability are indifference and blame. Team members may agree on team purpose, but when progress stalls, the team loses interest. Team members do not feel responsible enough to persevere through tough times. Teams can also fall into the practice of blaming outside people or circumstances for their lagging performance rather than challenging each other to help the team move forward. Indicators that show team commitment and accountability include developing clear and challenging goals, setting specific milestones, assigning team expectations for individual performance, and using regular and rigorous assessment of achievement.

Evaluation and celebration are important parts of establishing accountability in teams. If the team engages in regular assessment of its progress and process, it gains a sense of control and contribution. Assessment also allows for course correction before the team gets significantly off course. Celebration gives the team a feeling of achievement and closure. Without celebration, the team feels its work is never done, and no matter how important, the work becomes overwhelming and burdensome without evidence of success.

> A team cannot be indifferent about its purpose and be empowered at the same time.

Another important element of accountability is empowerment. Empowerment is an attitude toward taking on responsibility. Early attempts at empowerment focused on changing people's job descriptions and trying to articulate those areas where a person would be empowered. This approach turned out to be a hopeless task since the characteristic of work that gave rise to the need for empowerment was flexibility. Empowerment is not a list of what decisions a team can make or some specific delineation between responsibility and authority. It is, in fact, an ATTITUDE about confidence, risk, and commitment. It is the confidence of the team that it has the ability to do the work assigned, the willingness to try something new and take the consequences, a trust in the system that the team will not be "punished" for mistakes or innovation, and finally, the commitment to be involved enough to be empowered. A team cannot be indifferent about its purpose and be empowered at the same time.

Reflection

Use the Accountability Index on page 115 to reflect on your experiences with teams and accountability.

Team Work

Discuss accountability with a current team, using the accountability index dimensions as a guide.

Level of Accountability Index

Below are some indicators of the extent to which team members feel personally accountable for the results of the team. Consider a successful team you have been involved with in the past. Using the scale below, describe how team members viewed the team task. Now consider an unsuccessful team. Using a different pen, describe the team members on that team. Note where you see the differences. To what extent do you think these differences accounted for the success of the one team?

Goals:

1	3	5
Goals are general; individual responsibilities not articulated.	Some goals specified but few short-term milestones to gauge success.	Goals are clear with specific short-term indicators or progress.

Value to Organization:

1	3	5
Team task not tied to strategically important issues; has no sponsor.	Team task is generally recognized as important but not well structured.	Team task clearly seen as important across organization; membership is correct.

Perseverance:

1	3	5
Team work not valued as a way to accomplish work; expectations low.	Team work often starts strong but gets overrun by new events.	Results are expected; team seen as long-term commitment.

Empowerment:

1	3	5
Team sees itself as powerless; reluctant to take on difficult issues.	Team permission-oriented; seeks ways to minimize risk.	Team action-oriented; knows role; willing to experiment.

Celebration:

1	3	5
Team activity driven—satisfied with meeting and discussing.	Team desires success but has identified few measurable outcomes.	Team results driven; has specific outcomes; sees itself as responsible.

Dependability:

1	3	5
Team blames others when things go wrong; avoids self-assessment.	Team assigns responsibilities but allows non-performance; fears failure.	Team makes things happen; meets deadlines; continues to improve.

Team Charter

You may use the Team Charter in the appendix of the book to record your decisions about team accountability.

Trust

The final aspect of culture we are going to discuss is trust. For our discussion, trust is defined as being able to depend on each other. Effective teams develop a trusting culture of emotional safety in areas such as attribution of ideas, sharing of information, personal acceptance, and valued competence. In order for teams to engage in open discussion, there must be an atmosphere of trust in the team. For example, new ideas bring vulnerability. If new ideas are met with ridicule and/or skepticism, idea generation will soon dry up. Team members will decide it is not worth the risk to bring up a new idea, and they will remain silent.

The authors' experience is that trust is a prevailing issue for teams at all organizational levels. Teams indicate that they are concerned about trust, but they seldom know what to do about it. Since trust pervades all of the team's activities, internal and external, the issue needs to be regularly addressed and evaluated.

Information is an area around which trust often evolves. Team members are concerned that if they share information in the team, another team member may use it against them. For example, a team member might disclose that she or he has some extra human resource capacity in the short term, and another team member then tries to get those resources transferred to him or her in the long term. Or, the team has a preliminary brainstorming session to discuss how it might accomplish something, and at a later meeting a team member announces a specific decision and attributes it to the team. Both of these examples lead to distrust and an unwillingness to continue to share information. Without a willingness to share information, team meetings cease to have relevance, and the team becomes dysfunctional.

These same issues of trust apply to groups outside the team. If the team views those outside the team as suspect and less competent, and is unwilling to share information and trust others to deal with the information responsibly, it has little hope of being successful. Interdependence is such an integral characteristic of organizations today that if the team cannot trust it cannot operate. To rephrase an old adage, "no team is an island."

In order for teams to engage in open discussion, there must be an atmosphere of trust in the team.

Below are the elements that develop trust in a team. It is important to note that to develop trust, members of the team must also be trustworthy. Usually teams think of trust as a mysterious characteristic of a good team but something over which they have little control. They attribute lack of trust as belonging to others—we cannot trust our boss; those people in accounting don't trust us. Seldom do team members see the need for their own behavior to be trustworthy in order to engender trust. The more team members accept the primary responsibility for building trust, both within and outside the team, the easier and stronger trust will be.

TRUSTING BEHAVIORS

Openness	Willingly share information, ideas, thoughts, feelings, and reactions on issues under discussion.
Community	Offer materials and resources to help the team move ahead.
Empowerment	Allow the person to achieve the task in his or her own way.

TRUSTWORTHY BEHAVIORS

Respect	Recognize and communicate the strengths and abilities of others and believe that they have the capability to manage the situation at hand.

Cooperation	Lead the way in behaving cooperatively; put yourself in the other's position.
Dependability	Promise cautiously, and then keep your promises.

Reflection

How Does a Team Show Trust?		

Openness:

1	3	5
We seem to reach agreement but there is a lot of dissent outside meeting.	Discussion is guarded. Some issues surface but they are ones where positions are already known.	Ideas and concerns are shared without fear of vulnerability or ridicule.

Community:

1	3	5
Team members have primary allegiance outside team. Not willing to share.	Resources are shared only if specifically asked for and are usually given with some conditions attached.	Resources are seen as common to the team and to the organization. Need determines allocation.

Empowerment:

1	3	5
Team member contributions are second guessed and subject to team approval.	Minor issues are left to team member discretion though they are often open to scrutiny.	Team members are seen as competent and decisions only questioned on unusual issues.

Respect:

1	3	5
People outside team are seen as lacking understanding and skill; they are of little help.	Some people outside team are seen as capable but only if they have sponsors inside the team.	People outside team are seen as having valuable skills and information to contribute.

Cooperation:

1	3	5
First response to outside influence/information is defensive; team is suspicious.	Put many constraints on working with outsiders. "Need to know" used to protect information.	Volunteers to assist others. Does not see each assist requiring a payback.

Dependability:

1	3	5
Deliberately mislead others to protect advantage.	Sincere in making promises but will not maintain priority of request.	Promises made to others as important as to own team; keeps promises.

Team Work

With a current team, discuss the level of trust members have with each other and with those outside the team. What could the team do to improve those trust levels?

Team Charter

You may record your decisions about developing trust within the team in the Team Charter in the appendix of the book.

For a team to develop an internal atmosphere of trust there are some roles team members can consciously take on. These include:

- CATALYST—A person who brings out the best work of the team by exploring, building, and developing the ideas of others.
- CELEBRATOR—A person who uncovers and acknowledges things that team members do well; recognizes individual and team successes.
- SUPPORTER—A person who offers assistance to other team members and who nurtures and encourages people through difficult times.
- CONSTRUCTIVE CRITIC—A person who positively encourages team members to rethink ideas.
- AFFIRMER—A person who makes team members feel valued and increases team self-esteem.

Reflection

Recall a situation in which a team was highly active and reasonably effective. Who did you see playing these support roles on the team? How did the person go about playing this role? If you did not observe one of the roles, how might the team have benefited from someone taking on that role?

Role	*Who Plays This Role?*	*How Is Role Played?*
Catalyst		
Celebrator		
Supporter		
Constructive Critic		
Affirmer		

These support behaviors do not just naturally happen in teams. As part of the development of culture, the team needs to choose to develop these supportive roles. These roles can define individual relationships with other team members, or they can be collective roles for the team. If the team hopes to mature, it must address the issue of how it will support collective and individual growth and development in the team. Fulfilling these roles will allow the team to realize the potential within the team and to build a culture of trust and achievement.

Team Work

With a current team discuss these support roles and identify who in the team plays each role. If some role is left unclaimed, ask someone to take on the responsibility to play that role for a specific period of time. Then assess whether that role helped the trust and culture of the team.

How does a team know if it has created a positive culture? One way is to check how team members FEEL about their relationships within the team. Effective teams should engender the following feelings:

Inclusion	Feel valued as a member of the team; opinions sought; other team members respond to requests for help and are willing to share information.
Commitment	Team members are willing to make personal sacrifices to make sure that the team succeeds; they care about team results.
Loyalty	Team members show concern for the success of peers; they give each other the benefit of the doubt when problems arise; they look for members' strengths, not shortcomings.
Energy	Team members believe that what they do is important and tied to organizational goals; they have a strong orientation toward the future and expect to exceed their own current levels of performance.
Comfort	Team atmosphere is non-judgmental; there is an atmosphere of friendship and caring; feedback is sought and taken seriously as a chance to improve.
Trust	Team members do what they say they will; they defer to each other; they acknowledge one anothers' competence.
Fulfillment	Team members feel satisfied with the results of their efforts and that every team member is contributing equitably.

These culture indicators are part of the periodic assessment in the appendix of the book.

8

Rituals

Learning from this chapter:

- To understand why rituals are important to the effectiveness of a team.

- To identify those tasks, ground rules, and values for which rituals are appropriate.

- To be able to develop rituals that are meaningful and reinforcing.

- To assess the effectiveness of a ritual and be able to modify or abandon those that no longer serve their purpose.

Other things I want to learn about team rituals:

-
-

Rituals are dramatizations of the team's basic values. Rituals allow the unique characteristics of the team's culture to develop and endure. They reduce uncertainty and confusion in the team around key events and interactions. Without expressive events the team culture will die. Rituals allow the team to reinforce its identity. Rituals of social exchange govern relationships among members of the team and with those outside the team. Celebration rituals recognize milestones in the team's existence. Sometimes those milestones represent members entering or leaving the team. Sometimes the milestone is an accomplishment. Whatever the milestone, the team needs to find ways to acknowledge its occurrence. Rituals are especially important in today's work environment where we want teams to develop rapidly and be highly flexible, both in terms of task and membership. Rituals speed up the teaming process because they allow for the conscious shifting of gears within the team.

Rituals are dramatizations of the team's basic values.

In this chapter we will discuss rituals around four important dimensions of team life: adding members, losing members, ground rules, and celebrations. If a team develops rituals to help them manage the situations around these dimensions, they will find it easier to make progress and focus on desired results.

New Members

Bringing new members into the team is an important ritual in terms of maintaining team progress. Often when a new member joins a team, the person is left to his/her own devices to establish an appropriate role and become a contributing member of the team. The team will usually extend a greeting to the new team member but often actual orientation tends to be superficial. To effectively entrench a new member, the team must:

Reestablish Its Purpose   The new team member needs to understand why the team exists and what it hopes to accomplish. The new team member also must be brought up to speed on the current state of discussion within the team. The new person especially needs to be clear about issues that have been addressed and closed and those that are open for discussion. It is disheartening for a new team member to be told at a team meeting that his or her ideas have already been discussed and rejected.

Provide Social Information   The new team member needs to receive social information about the team. As teams develop they establish a history and collect memories. The more history, the harder it is for a new member to join the group. The team has jargon, inside stories, and well-developed taboos that the new member has to interpret. Without rituals for new membership, it may take the new member such a long time to become an "insider" that the team has lost the value of new input. Also, if there is not a new member ritual, the new member may always feel like an outsider and never develop the commitment expected from the established team. If new members come into the team with any frequency, this lack of commitment will eventually become the norm and destroy the team.

Rituals are especially important in today's work environment where we want teams to develop rapidly and be highly flexible both in terms of task and membership.

There are a number of ways that teams can bring new members into the team. Some teams create a "mentor" for the new team member. The mentor's role is to teach the person about the politics of the team. This includes providing information on past discussions and the things that different team members feel are important; defining any jargon and inside jokes the new member does not understand; and assuring that the new member is included in discussion and given a role to play in the work of the team.

Another orientation ritual, which the author observed at a large organization where membership changed with some frequency, focused around the purpose of the team. When the team established its purpose, it had individual pictures taken of team members. The pictures encircled a written statement of team purpose, and under each picture was a role and commitment statement for that member. The display hung in the team meeting room. When a new member came into the group the team members introduced themselves, discussed the team purpose and then their individual commitment to the team. When the new person had been with the team for about a month, the person's picture was added and he or she was asked to make his/her own commitment to the team. The picture on the wall reminded team members why they were there and also helped the new member get to know the members of the team. The ritual was well enough defined that it did not take an inordinate amount of time to complete, and additionally, it provided a useful process/progress check to the team.

Teams in today's organizations often need to bring in temporary team members. These members may be technical experts, people responsible for improving the skill base of the team, or even members of another team who will be partners on a project. Even short-term members need a membership ritual. The more the team can help the new entrant understand the work of the team and the expectations for this new addition, the more quickly the team will reap the benefit of the addition.

Roles and Responsibilities   Teams need to discuss the role of the new team member. The team changes with the addition of each new member. The dynamics of the team will shift. This is neither good nor bad; it just is a reality. Team members need to address the changes that have taken place. They need to decide how best to capitalize on the skills and perspective of the new member, and the new member needs to feel she or he can make a unique and important contribution to the team.

Ground Rules   An important part of an initiation ritual is to share the ground rules and norms of the team with the new member. Just as each person in the original team came with differing expectations for membership, so does the new team member. If the team has been in existence for a long period of time, some of the norms are probably taken for granted. Explaining the "rules of the road" to a new member can raise the team's awareness of how it operates.

To the extent that the team can use this time to re-examine its rules and culture rather than just preach to the new member, the ritual will increase in value. A characteristic of effective, long-term teams is that they are able to renew themselves. Each time the team examines and challenges its rules and norms in an open-minded manner it allows for team renewal. Bringing a new member onto the team is a natural time for the team to do a renewal assessment.

Changes in team membership cannot be left unaddressed. Teams often struggle with membership change because they do not address the change in a straightforward manner, but rather they allow the change to exist as an undercurrent. The result is a feeling of being adrift and a lessening of common purpose, which undermines the commitment of the team.

Reflection

What rituals have you experienced when you have joined a team? _____
_____

How were these rituals helpful? _____

What would have made them more effective? _____
_____

Member Exit

Because each team member makes a unique contribution to the composition and capability of the team, the team needs to assess the impact of a team member's leaving. Sometimes the person leaving will have played a vital role. Then the team must carefully assess both the process and task skills they will need to replace. They may look for some of those skills if they have the ability to choose the replacement team member. They may decide that this vacancy presents an opportunity for learning for current members of the team. On the other hand, the person leaving the team may have been a poor match. In this case the team needs to talk about how they will work differently now that the team member is gone. In this kind of discussion, it is important to focus on the behaviors and skills of the departing team member, not the personality. The team needs to consider the dynamic of the team as a whole and how each member contributed to the problems of the team. It is easy at this point to blame the departing team member for the entire mismatch and to assume, or at least hope, that the new team member will "fix" the situation. This fantasy denies the team an important opportunity for self-reflection and places a very heavy burden on the new member.

Reflection

What rituals have you experienced when someone has left a team? _____

_____

How were these rituals helpful? _____

What would have made them more effective? _____

_____

Each team needs to define the rituals that make sense to them.

Sometimes the entire team will be disbanded. At a large organization well-known for frequent restructuring, a team that had been together for three years found itself in this situation. The function the team represented was being re-engineered, and the team members were being dispersed to process teams in the organization. The team had worked very well together and had accomplished a great deal. In fact, their effectiveness had so raised their perceived value in the organization that management felt they could be even more valuable if they were part of their "customer" teams. It was with mixed feelings of accomplishment and sadness that the team prepared to disband. Team members decided they needed a ritual to bring their work to an end and to set the expectations for the next stage of their personal and professional development. So they decided to have a wake.

The team rented a hotel meeting room, a coffin, and other trappings associated with funerals. Each team member prepared a eulogy for a fellow team member, focusing on the value and achievement that person brought to the team. The ceremony reflected a belief in reincarnation as each team member included a vision of the next life in his or her eulogy. They filled the coffin with items that represented the team's way of doing things to demonstrate that they had to be open to the ways of their new teams. When the ceremony was over, they had a party.

For this team, the ritual of a wake was very valuable. But the lesson to be learned from this is not to have a wake when a team disbands, but rather to show how important it is to provide an opportunity for the team to address change. A ritual around a team change can provide security during unwanted transitions. However, rituals cannot be prescriptive. Imagine telling a team they needed to have a wake. The team would think the idea ludicrous and would undoubtedly resist. Each team needs to define the rituals that make sense to them.

Work Rituals

Rituals also occur around day-to-day activities. Since these rituals are so frequent, they are often very powerful. Often work method rituals demonstrate how serious the team is about its ground rules. For example, if the team says that it is important to begin meetings on time but it seldom happens, there is little meaning to the ground rule. Teams serious about starting on time often have rituals associated with late arrivals. Some are as simple as beginning the meeting promptly and not waiting for latecomers, no matter who they are. Other ground rules are more humorous. One team that often described itself as "menu driven" would require the last arriving member to bring donuts to the next meeting. Another team assessed people $1 for each minute they were late. Needless to say, this demonstrated that the team was serious about starting on time. The money was collected over a period of time and then the team either donated it to a charity or used it for a team function—sometimes for training a team member.

Reflection

What rituals have you experienced around team ground rules? _____

_____

How were these rituals helpful? _____

_____

What would have made them more effective? _____

_____

Many of the process values we have discussed are greatly enforced if they have rituals attached to them. If, for example, the team says it values input from all members of the team, then it needs to create a process for assuring that it happens. One team the author knows begins the discussion of a given topic by going around the meeting table and asking each person to give their facts and feelings about the topic before the general discussion begins. Another option might be to assign positions about the topic beforehand and have people collect information to support that position. As with the other rituals, they need to come from the team and make sense to how the team operates. The adage that "actions speak louder than words" is appropriate to rituals around work methods. Unless the team consciously creates rituals that reinforce what they say is important to them, those values will languish.

Celebration

In fact, teams usually celebrate too seldom rather than too frequently.

Organizations often focus on problems and challenges and thus forget to celebrate achievements along the way. Celebrations provide the team with endurance and sustainability. If the team only faces problems, its work becomes burdensome.

The foundation for celebration needs to come from the purposing process described in Chapter 3. As the team defines its purpose and sets its goals, it also develops measures for success. When those measures are achieved, the team needs to celebrate.

Over the years, research has provided information about how to make rewards effective. In order for team celebrations to be effective, they too must follow these general principles. First, the celebration/reward must be closely tied to the work of the team. It must be clear that the achievement was the result of team effort and not caused by some external force. False celebrations will only undermine the team's self-confidence.

Second, celebrations need to be timely. To simply be recognized at the annual awards banquet will not give the team a sufficient sense of accomplishment. Celebrations need to be event driven, not calendar driven. When the team has reached a goal or managed a difficult problem, it is time to celebrate. Teams need not be afraid of over celebrating. As long as the celebration represents a true accomplishment it is appropriate. In fact, teams usually celebrate too seldom rather than too frequently.

The third important point about rewards is that the celebration must reflect the level of accomplishment. For example, the celebration might be as simple as a time at the beginning of a team meeting to discuss achievements since the last meeting, or to recognize the good work of one of the members. The achievement might warrant getting together for a pizza lunch or other treat. Perhaps the recognition needs to be wider and the team could have its picture and an article in the company newsletter. The greater the accomplishment, the greater the reward should be.

The key is to have the reward be important to the team. How does this team like to celebrate? As an example, there was a team of engineers in a large manufacturing organization who gave each other personal recognition by passing a huge stuffed emu among the group. One of the team members had won the stuffed toy at the local state fair and it became the mascot of the team. It became a team ritual that when an individual within the team did something noteworthy or helpful, she or he got the bird. Sometimes the bird stayed in one place for days, sometimes only for hours. The general manager learned that his job was just to look and see if the bird had moved and then inquire about the success it represented.

This example again represents how team-specific rituals must be. They cannot be prescribed by outsiders. They tend to evolve with the development of the team. It is important that the team develop its own rituals that mark the milestone of the work and membership.

Reflection

What rituals have you experienced around celebrating achievements? _____

_____

How were these rituals helpful? _____

_____

What would have made them more effective? _____

_____

Team Work

Discuss with current team members what kind of rituals would be helpful to your team. Consider the following questions:

1. What rituals do you currently use?
2. Are they appropriate?
3. How could they be improved?
4. Around which team dimensions and ground rules do you need to establish rituals?
5. Describe what you might do:

_____

_____

_____

Team Charter

You may record your discussion points and decisions about rituals in the Team Charter in the appendix of the book.

CHAPTER

Learning

Learning from this chapter:

- To understand the role of learning in the development of a team.

- To be able to identify the key dimensions of learning for a team.

- To understand the positive aspects of contention and how to use it within a team to improve performance.

- To be able to recognize the different elements of diversity within a team and how they influence how the team operates.

- To identify the characteristics of a creative team.

Other things I want to learn about team learning:

-
-

This chapter generally discusses the development of a team culture that allows the team to grow and develop. Learning is the process that a team uses to continually improve the way it performs. The team grows as it builds its capacity to think and behave in new ways.

The need for ongoing learning in organizations has gained attention because of the incredible changes in technology and markets that are driving business today. Peter Senge in his book *The Fifth Discipline* (Senge, 1990) sets forth an articulate and comprehensive view of learning. Senge asserts that there is a need to tie individual development with organizational performance and that development is an ongoing process that emphasizes self-sustaining performance, not simply single project performance. To create a learning culture, the organization must have mechanisms to continually upgrade the competencies of its people.

Learning is the process that a team uses to continually improve the way it performs.

Teams are the best current mechanisms organizations have for continued organizational learning. Developing individual competencies in isolation will not meet the complex needs of the organization. The organization can create individual cells of excellence, but if they do not communicate and work together, their contribution is limited. Teams allow the organization to create the shared knowledge and understanding needed to continually improve and to move quickly in the face of change. Also, teams can provide the climate and support needed for the challenge of organizational renewal.

Team learning goes beyond team building which tends to focus on interpersonal skill development. A team with a learning culture fosters both individual and group development. Team learning addresses how the team thinks, as well as improving interaction and problem-solving skills. In the following sections we will discuss three important aspects of team learning: (1) conflict, (2) diversity, and (3) thinking skills.

Conflict

Learning requires that the team be constantly changing and adjusting its mindset. Therefore, the team must enhance its ability to think and behave in new ways. One of the keys to gaining this behavioral flexibility is the willingness to deal with the conflict that accompanies change. The adage that "a good team is a team that agrees" is not only inaccurate, but is probably dangerous in today's work environment. Teams need to seek and accept conflicting views as a natural and necessary part of a group of unique people getting together to address complex issues and opportunities. Perhaps a better adage to guide a team is "if two of us always agree, one of us is not necessary."

In Chapter 12 we will discuss some of the basic skills needed for conflict resolution within teams. However, the team will not develop or use whatever conflict management skills it acquires unless it has a team culture that says that conflict adds to the potential of the team.

The more successful and cohesive the team, the harder it is to challenge the current mindset.

The team needs to define its attitude towards conflict in two areas: variance and consistency. How important is it to the team to follow the traditions of the organization; to come up with decisions and solutions that fit into the way things are currently done? Teams are likely to give a quick answer that they, of course, are looking for new ways to do things. However, the team needs to investigate its commitment to this attitude to be sure it truly reflects the feelings of the group. Once confirmed, the team then needs to learn skills and set ground rules to assure this willingness to do things differently prevails over time.

The team must be explicit about its commitment to "turn things upside down," or it will be frustrated by the pressure to conform to current thinking and traditional solutions.

Variances are often viewed as indications that things are going wrong in the organization. For example, if there is a budget variance, the unit is expected to "bring it into line" or if someone does not follow a set procedure, it is viewed as a mistake. The assumption fundamental to a variance is that something is in error. Since teams are often charged with investigating problems, it is vital that they change their views on variances. Variances are indicators that something is DIFFERENT from what was expected but not necessarily bad.

To be able to learn from organizational problems, the team needs to strive to understand the issues they are addressing, not just try to get them back to a previous or predetermined state. Returning to "normal" will not resolve underlying issues and foster change. It will only cover up issues. Suspending judgment while seeking out various perspectives for any issue is the first step BEFORE taking action.

Reflection

What ground rules have you seen used that focus on assuring that different points of view surface? _____

_____

_____

How were these ground rules effective? _____

_____

What would have made them more effective? _____

_____

_____

A recent, well-researched challenge to the need for consistency within organizations comes from Richard Tanner Pascale (Pascale, 1990). His work deals with the need for change and contention in the organization. Pascale tracked various successful organizations to see if and how they maintained their success. He found that it was indeed very difficult for successful organizations to stay successful. As soon as the organization began to work well, it began to lock into its approaches. The organization began to think that it knew the right way to do things and stopped exploring new alternatives. The more successful the organization, the harder it was for it to challenge the current paradigm.

This study on organizations has a parallel in teams. The more successful and cohesive the team, the harder it is to challenge the current mindset. Successful teams desperately need to foster contention and challenge assumptions to renew the team's thinking and allow it to learn.

Irving Janis (Janis, 1972), in his work on groupthink, also expressed concern for a team's need for agreement. In groupthink, agreement within the team is valued more than team effectiveness. The team will discourage, and to the extreme, isolate team members who do not go along with the majority. The result is that team members simply accede to each other's statements, avoid bringing up controversial issues and different perspectives, and keep concerns to themselves. This kind of thinking often results in a team of very capable people making very serious mistakes. To outsiders the team appears incompetent. Incompetence is usually not the issue; not exploring differing perspectives usually is. The team denies itself the resource of new information and views and reinforces its narrow perspective. Later we will discuss groupthink in more detail and consider team strategies to avoid falling into this trap.

The cultural issues around contention, then, stem from the willingness of the team to learn by drawing out, tolerating, and exploring different ideas from the team. To the extent that it is acceptable for members of the team to hold different opinions, the team will consider multiple alternatives and be willing to be at variance with tradition. To the extent that members of the team feel the need to agree, the less it will tolerate discussion of divergent ideas, and the more likely the team's "new" ideas will look like "old" ideas. Teams need to foster and reward those people who creatively put them off track. The capability the team needs to develop is the pursuit of relentless questioning while still retaining focus.

Team Charter

You can record your discussion and decisions on the ground rules that you think will help your team develop a culture that is accepting of conflict in the Team Charter in the appendix of the book.

Diversity

One of the sources for conflict in a team is diversity in membership. Few countries have the cultural diversity of the US, and teams within US organizations reflect this diversity. As with most team issues, there are tradeoffs in having diverse teams. In general, diverse teams are more innovative in their ideas because they draw from multiple perspectives on issues. However, the diversity within the team often makes it difficult to draw out and use those different perspectives. Some examples of the kind of diversity issues that teams need to address include:

Individualism vs. Collectivism   Members of a team will be dispersed along an individualism-collectivism culture continuum. Those near the individualism end of the continuum operate with loose ties to others; people are expected to look after their own interests. These individualists will seek individual achievement and recognition and may have trouble accepting team goals as their own. At the other end of the continuum, collectivism, we find people whose culture values the ties between people. For these team members, each person is expected to look after members of the group and to hold the beliefs and opinions of the group. Self-interest is subordinate to team interest. Team recognition is adequate reward for people who are collectivist.

For teams, these preferences for individualism and collectivism mean finding ways for some team members to differentiate themselves while still working for team goals and accepting team accountability. Conflict arises between these two cultural styles when the individualists push for their way. The team-oriented members are likely to give in to the individualists, but usually at the expense of commitment to the team. The team begins to lose its meaning and is seen as simply a platform for individual views. As the team establishes its culture, it needs to decide how to meet team member needs for individuality and cohesion.

Conflict and Compliance   Members of the team will also fall on a continuum with regard to conflict and compliance. To people who value compliance, the harmony of the team is a primary and essential element of team protocol. Conformity is expected and open conflict highly frowned upon. For those team members who enjoy, or at least accept conflict, their focus will be on voicing contrary views and fostering competition. They often enjoy argument for the sake of argument.

Risk avoidance is also a facet of the conflict/compliance continuum. Compliance and risk aversion are often companions in team behavior. To avoid conflict, team members will sidestep controversial issues or settle for solutions that comply with traditional mindsets. This risk avoidance is often a serious problem for teams since the majority of the population tends toward the compliance side of the continuum.

Teams must find ways to allow members less comfortable with open conflict to voice their opinions and concerns. If the contention becomes too heated, these members will withdraw. The more the team can build conflict and contention around the discussion of different perspectives on issues rather than volume of voice or personal affronts, the easier it is for all to contribute.

Power and Hierarchy   Another diversity factor which influences team process is the willingness of team members to accept position power and hierarchy. Some members of the team will show great respect for position power and feel uncomfortable challenging authority. They are more willing to accept the leader's decision and to follow organizational rules. Other team members view the team and the organization from a more egalitarian view. They resist seeking permission to take initiative and do not automatically accept management prerogatives.

Having team members with differing views on power and hierarchy can derail the search for resolutions to problems. Teams that are willing to follow more than one solution pathway at a time have an easier time with this aspect of diversity. Those team members who are reluctant to work outside the current organizational paradigm can follow the more conservative options the team has identified, while those more rebellious can follow more perilous paths.

Teams must find ways to allow members less comfortable with open conflict to voice their opinions and concerns.

Diverse teams take more time in start-up, but they make up for it with creativity and ease of implementation.

Diverse groups are clearly more challenging to bring together as teams than are homogeneous groups.

Participation is not easy for those who value hierarchy. They often feel inadequate in the role of decision maker and think that it is the bosses' right and responsibility to solve the organization's problems. The team needs to help these team members see that their perspectives and skills are necessary for continuous organization and team improvement. The team must create a safe environment for presenting ideas.

Reflection

Diversity Self-Assessment						

Plot yourself on the following continuum to determine what individual characteristics you bring to a team:

	1	2	3	4	5	
Structured	1	2	3	4	5	Flexible
Collective	1	2	3	4	5	Individual
Right Way	1	2	3	4	5	Many Ways
Security	1	2	3	4	5	Ambiguity
Cautious	1	2	3	4	5	Risky
Confront	1	2	3	4	5	Agree
Hierarchy	1	2	3	4	5	Egalitarian
Expressive	1	2	3	4	5	Reserved
Traditional	1	2	3	4	5	Experimental
Logical	1	2	3	4	5	Intuitive
Formal	1	2	3	4	5	Informal

Diverse groups are clearly more challenging to bring together as teams than are homogeneous groups. Cultural differences exaggerate the normal team differences around confrontation, verbal assertion, leadership, and risk. Because there is likely to be great variance around the cultural backgrounds and style preferences of team members, it becomes very important that each member of the team have an opportunity to express his or her expectations of teamwork. It is also important that the team allow for a wide range of behaviors and roles in the team.

However difficult they are to pull together, diverse teams offer the best return on an investment of organizational effort and time. Because of their differences in approach, opinions, and values, diverse teams have the ability to view issues from many perspectives. When it comes time to implement ideas, these teams tend to have more workable solutions and a better idea of the resistance that the new idea will face. Diverse teams take more time in start-up, but they make up for it with creativity and ease of implementation.

Team Work

When you and your teammates have completed your self-assessments, plot all of your scores on the team scoring form in the appendix, using a different color for each person. Note where there are big gaps between different members of the team. These are areas where the team can work to be sure that diversity is an asset and not a liability to the working of the team.

Creativity

One of the primary reasons organizations are interested in forming teams is to tap into creative group synergy. Creativity is defined as seeing the same things as others see but in different ways. Creativity as a part of team culture does not revolve around product or service innovation as much as around attitude. Is the team willing to consider new ideas; to go beyond the conventional way of doing things? The creativity that is most useful to organizations is imagination—the ability to see the possible.

Earlier in the book we dealt with some of the techniques that encourage creativity and new thinking. The process of dialogue is especially important to creativity. However, as was the case in the discussion of controversy, technique alone is not enough. If the culture of the team is not receptive to creativity, the seeds of enlightened techniques like dialogue will lay fallow. A willingness to be creative gives the team energy. Without it, team discussion tends to plow old ground, and solutions are fixed in how things have been done in the past.

Given the pressure in the organization to follow current mindsets, the team must foster an attitude of creativity within its boundaries if it is going to be effective.

Recent work on teams in the Phoenix Fire Department showed that the most successful teams were those given assignments for which there were no current solutions or rules and regulations (Kime, 1995). Where teams were asked to address ongoing organizational issues, they were reluctant to go beyond the current approaches. They tried to find solutions within the current paradigm. Those teams often ended up frustrated because those in the old systems were not willing to change in any but the most minor ways. After a period of time, the teams would simply say they could not achieve their goals because they could not change the policy, or they could not get others to help them.

However, the teams within the fire department that were charged with developing new areas of service, or to develop new ways to work together, had a great deal of success. They did not encounter the same policy or people obstacles, though they were governed by the same regulations and organizational traditions. Because they were not burdened by how things were done in the past, they were able to be creative.

The fire department example shows how important it is for teams to break out of old mindsets and look for new ways to see things. Bringing up the same approaches and solutions gives the team little sense of progress and the team loses momentum. Most organizations create teams to bring new life into old processes, or to have a new look at organizational issues. However, given the pressure in the organization to follow current mindsets, the team must foster an attitude of creativity within its boundaries if it is going to be effective. Teams cannot get transformational results without transformational thinking.

Reflection

How Creative Is Your Team?		
Creative Characteristic	*Who on Your Team Does This?*	*What Is the Impact on the Team?*
Provides lots of ideas.		
Draws out multiple alternatives.		
Is comfortable dealing with abstract ideas.		
Challenges assumptions the team makes.		
Asks "why?" and "why not?"		
Provides the team with objective facts.		
Shares feelings and gut reactions.		
Is optimistic—finds ways for things to work.		
Is realistic—helps team learn from mistakes.		
Suggests unorthodox ways to handle issues.		
Sees failure as a means of learning.		
Consciously gets the team to go outside its mindset.		
Talks through ideas; gives step-by-step pathway.		
Identifies critical factors for success of idea.		

How does a team go from a place where team members are afraid to take risks to a place where it is safe to propose new ideas? There are a few general guidelines:

- **Delay.** Delay often carries a negative connotation in team work. However, with creativity it can breathe life into an idea. Rather than grasp for a quick answer, the team pauses and tries to understand and add to its options. Group decision making is by a tendency to accept the first reasonable solution brought to the table. In order to be creative, the team needs to thoughtfully explore many alternatives before choosing the ones to pursue.

- **Absence of judgment.** Ridicule within the team cannot be tolerated. Remarks that demean or chastise a person will cause all team members to withdraw from the discussion. Teams that develop a culture for attacking people and ideas will have fewer and fewer ideas to discuss. However, a constructive critic can be very helpful. Constructive critics focus on ideas, not people. Ideas are neither good nor bad at inception. Discussion needs to focus on how to make something work rather than on why it won't work.

- **Confidence to share an idea.** This comes from the self-esteem created when team members pay attention to another teammate's idea and explore its possibilities, whether or not it is ultimately accepted. Confidence also comes from celebrating team successes.

- **Attentiveness.** Most ideas are lost in the process of team discussion. Team members give suggestions and they fall on deaf ears. Everyone is pushing his or her own idea and not listening to the ideas of others. Team members must move away from this egocentric attitude and develop the ability to focus on what others say. Teams that take time to explore ideas have a much better chance for creative solutions. Building on the ideas of others is a key creativity tool.

- **Dialogue.** Ideas are seldom presented in finished form. Often just a concept is presented. To flesh out an idea requires a serious exchange of information and feelings. To engage in dialogue requires the team to sharpen thinking, conversation, and interpersonal skills.

A reason why organizations need to foster teams is that the cultural supports for creativity are much easier to develop in a team than they are in a large organization. Feelings of value and importance are difficult to maintain in groups of one thousand. Ideas often remain undeveloped in large departments. Teams of 10 or 12 can be much more supportive than organizations. Inspiration is fragile; teams are best able to kindle its spark.

Part III

Conclusion

Developing a performance culture is important and ongoing work for a team. Because culture is not easily observable, teams sometimes have difficulty addressing the issue of culture. However, if the team looks at culture as the manifestation of the team's purpose and the demonstration of its ground rules, the team can create specific behaviors to develop a strong performance culture. That culture will allow the team to gel and capture its true potential.

Since culture is an enduring team characteristic, the team needs to monitor it and nurture its desired behaviors on a regular basis. In the periodic review instruments in the appendix to the book, you will find assessment tools for measuring different aspects of team culture. The assessment tools are to be used in conjunction with the Team Charter to provide an ongoing measure of the strengths and weaknesses of the team's culture.

End of Section Activities

Discussion Questions

1. Describe and give the implications for having a team with a high performance culture.
2. Compare and contrast the performance values of commitment and accountability.
3. Explain why trust is important to a team. How would you determine if a team was performing with a high level of trust?
4. Using a well-known and established event (the Olympics or another major sports event; a presidential election; the Academy awards; graduation from college; a religious rite; etc.), describe the rituals around these events. What do the rituals emphasize? Have the rituals changed over time? How? Why? How important are these rituals to the event? What would happen if you took the rituals away?
5. Explain why conflict is important to a team. Which elements of conflict should a team foster? Give an example of an effective use of conflict in a team.
6. Considering a group you belong to, describe the ways in which the group is diverse. Describe how these dimensions of diversity might affect team performance.
7. Explain why creativity is an element of team culture and not just a technique for decision making.

Application: Critical Incidents

1. You are about to meet with the Ledger Task Force to try and get the team to recommend accounting changes in manufacturing sales, credit, and accounting so that all the ledgers contain the same codes and mesh together for month-end and year-end closings. This is the first time this group has met, but it is not the first Ledger Task Force. For about two years the accounting department has been trying to get the different parts of the company to come together under a common ledger. Task forces get started but then fizzle because there is so much resistance in the organization and because the CEO does not view internal financial issues as all that important.

You have been given the job of Chair of the Task Force. The new CFO is adamant about finally getting this ledger business completed. The team members have been drawn from all the areas of accounting, and there is a representative from MIS. Your first task will be to get all the departments within the company to agree to the same set of object codes or account descriptions and to a definition of what is included in each. Manufacturing and sales have been working for years from their own codes. Their codes are configured to meet their individual needs but do not match each other, or the accounting codes necessary to integrate all accounting information. Therefore, the end-of-the-month report requires a great deal of manual re-input of data, and you are never sure that you have captured and combined the right information.

You are concerned that this task force will meet with the same fate as the past ones—death by indifference. A number of the members have already questioned why the group is coming together again. They all know that it is absolutely necessary to complete this task. As the company continues to grow, having multiple ledgers becomes an ever increasing nightmare. However, they are not at all sure they are the ones to handle the change.

What will you do to help the team become committed to the task and take responsibility for this project?

2. You are a member of an Emergency Services management team for a large city. The management team has representatives from various constituencies in the emergency services delivery business including hospitals, urgent care centers, ambulance service, and the fire department. With the growth in the city, the changes in medical service delivery systems, and changes in payment criteria, the emergency services sector is under great pressure to change the way it provides service.

Up to this point the management team has primarily acted as a mechanism for sharing information. Each of the entities managed their own units, and except when necessary, stayed out of each other's way. The increasing demand for service will not permit this kind of detached action. Providers of emergency services need to work together if they are going to be able to meet the service demand and maintain cost levels. Providers in many other cities have been driven out of business because they did not respond to the changes.

You have just finished the monthly meeting of the management team. Everyone voiced the need to work together but there was the same guarded and defensive discussion that usually occurred. Each member of the team is afraid to give up any service or decision-making authority because they are afraid they will be replaced by another provider. You can see people drawing lines around their specialties and responsibilities and building walls between each other.

As the city's representative on the team, you feel responsible to hold the group together and get them to agree to changes that will meet the service needs of the community. What can you do to build trust among the group so that they can find ways to improve service and work together?

3. You are Chairman of the Board of a company that is going through incredible change. The company has been in existence for many years, and until recently, has been family held. However, the opportunity to grow globally convinced the family to seek outside funds through an IPO.

Taking the company public put enormous pressure on the Board. Some of the family Board members are not able nor interested in managing such a complex company. Outside investors are requiring a more professional Board. However, you have great concerns for maintaining the stability of the company. What measures can you take to be sure that the Board does not lose the support of the family as some of the family Board members leave, and that new Board members coming in understand the culture and interests of the company?

4. You are the new superintendent of a large school district. The district is viewed as providing a good education, but is seen as relatively traditional. You know that the changes taking place in the educational arena are going to stress the district to maintain its quality reputation.

Your predecessor was a good administrator. He came to the district when it was young, and for twenty years, he guided it to its current level. He knew everything there was to know about the district and made virtually all the decisions. While the district did well under his care, it is unlikely that such a tight rein will work in the future. There are just too many changes underfoot. You are going to need all the input and energy you can find. Besides, authoritarian leadership has never been your style. Your success has come from empowering your staff and playing the role of coach.

Your dilemma is your executive staff. They are very able people, but most of them served for many years under the past administrator. They are used to having the decisions made in the Superintendent's office. When you have staff meetings, they are agreeable but offer few suggestions. You have tried to generate discussion by throwing out some wild ideas. The staff looks at you warily and says if that is what you want they will give it a try. However, there is very little action between staff meetings.

You would like the group to be more confrontive; to throw out ideas and wrestle with them. You would like to see them define a future district much different from the one they maintain today. You know they have good ideas and that they care very much about the district and their profession. How can you get them to challenge the status quo?

Reinforcement: Exercises

OBSERVATION

Attend a staff meeting of which you are not a member, or attend a public meeting, and see if you can identify what rituals the team observes. Pay particular attention to opening, closing, and rituals that keep order or move the meeting along.

OBSERVATION

Interview a person from another team. Ask them to describe the rituals that they use within their team.

1. Was the person aware of the rituals before you brought them to his/her attention?

_____

2. Do the rituals seem to be effective? _____

3. What could you borrow from their rituals to use in your own team?

_____

_____

Constructive Controversy in Action

OBSERVATION

Using the assessment form below, evaluate a team meeting to see how well the members engage in behaviors that lead to constructive controversy. Make a tick mark each time you hear a constructive conflict behavior demonstrated.

Behavior	*Frequency*	*Comments*
Disagreement around issues initiated.		
Multiple perspectives on issue presented.		
Active listening—paraphrasing of a position.		
Competence of opposing view acknowledged.		
Acceptance of new ideas shown by reconceptualizing issue.		
Uncertainty about correctness of own position expressed.		
Discussion moved laterally to take in peripheral issues; sequence or logic not emphasized.		
Clarification questions used to clarify issue and explore options.		
Assumptions about issue challenged.		
New ideas recognized and explored without judgment.		

How well did the team you observed perform? Were team members able to use a variety of constructive controversy behaviors? How could they improve their discussion?

Reinforcement: Understanding Values

As a team, complete the following steps:

1. Collectively identify common values in an organization. These values might include things like honesty, hard work, friendliness, loyalty, conflict, etc. Brainstorm until your list has 25 to 30 values.
2. From the list, select the five that are most important to you and put them in the pyramid below. Do this selection and recording individually.
3. As a group, complete the team section of the pyramid, selecting those values that are important to you as a team.
4. Now, as a group, complete the organization section of the pyramid, selecting those values that are important to the organization as a whole.

5. Discuss the difference in values at different levels of the organization.
   a. What does the team value that the organization does not? How can the team get the organization to see that this value is important? What can the team do to be sure that this difference does not get in the way of its success?
   b. What does the organization value that the team does not? Will these value differences cause the team difficulty in getting the organization to accept its decisions or work processes?
   c. How do individual team member values differ from team values and organization values? How can the team resolve these value differences?

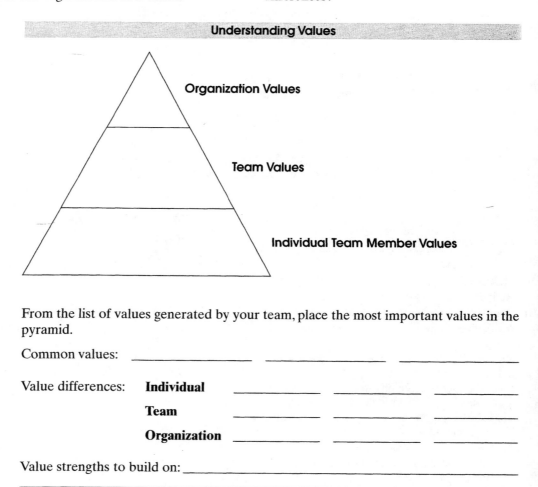

Understanding Values

Organization Values

Team Values

Individual Team Member Values

From the list of values generated by your team, place the most important values in the pyramid.

Common values: _____ _____ _____

Value differences: **Individual**   _____ _____ _____

                                Team   _____ _____ _____

                                  Organization   _____ _____ _____

Value strengths to build on: _____

_____

Value issues to resolve: _____

_____

PART

IV

Politics and Advancing Team Renewal

Learning from this section:

■ To understand the importance of influencing skills in organizations.

■ To be able to differentiate between internal and external political strategies.

■ To select assessment tools for team evaluation and renewal.

Other things that I want to learn about politics and team renewal:

■

■

"Positive politicking" is necessary for teams to work together effectively.

This final section deals with the notion of problem solving and assessment as continuous improvement mechanisms for the team. Problem solving is addressed first from within the team (internal politics), then from outside the team (external politics). Politics often has a negative meaning within organizations. However, for teams, it means having the organizational savvy to get your ideas and recommendations accepted. Without engaging in "positive politicking" teams often feel frustrated and manipulated by the management of the organization and community. The team often spends a great deal of time and energy working on issues only to find an unaccepted or disinterested audience. The effective use of politics means appreciating and addressing problems from every possible perspective, and then communicating the resulting solutions in a way that meets every constituent's need.

Teams experience conflict because it is not easy for people to work together. That everything has not gone perfectly during the development cycle of forming and identifying goals and plans of action, is therefore not surprising.

Conflict is good and often necessary to the quest for effectiveness. Other tools are needed as well and at many levels to improve and measure team processes and products. As teams work through problems and evaluate their tasks, it is only natural that the cycle would kick back to the beginning with renewal measures.

In this section we will discuss the importance of politics to the team process, how to solve problems that are created from internal and external influences, and finally how to measure progress and outcomes. The goal of this section is to synthesize all of the information in previous chapters and illustrate the continuing cycle of team development—from structure, process, culture, politics, and evaluation. It is this evaluation process that either brings closure to a one-task-only team, or renews teams that will continue to work together over a period of time. In the case of the evolving team, assessment measures are used to improve the next structure, process, culture, politics, and assessment project.

10

Internal Politics
and Implementation

Learning from this chapter:

■ To detail the problem-solving process.

■ To explain reasons for conflict internal to teams.

■ To identify strategies for overcoming obstacles to effectiveness.

■ To identify specific skills and attitudes needed to address internal conflict.

Other things I want to learn about politics within a team and organization:

■

■

Purpose

The purpose of this chapter is to focus on making the team's work implementable. Activities must be effective and efficient. This chapter will address skills needed to solve problems within the team, because teams experience a drain on energy when there are negative undercurrents. Before we examine the primary skills used in problem solving and politics, we should look at the causes of conflict. While the causes may not be the same universally, there are some common categories of conflict that we see when working in teams. Many of the tools and skills of using politics within the team and organization may also be used at a more comprehensive level. The external environment will be addressed in Chapter 11.

Good politics is the art of meeting members' needs as well as of solving problems and communicating recommendations.

The problem-solving process applies to managing the internal and external influences on the team. Remember that part of good politics is the art of solving problems and communicating recommendations in a way that meets each constituent's needs. The problem-solving process is closely tied to goal setting and is one of the key purposes for teams. Figure 10.1 represents the science of problem solving, or the steps for achieving a solution. The way in which these steps are achieved, through sensitivity and

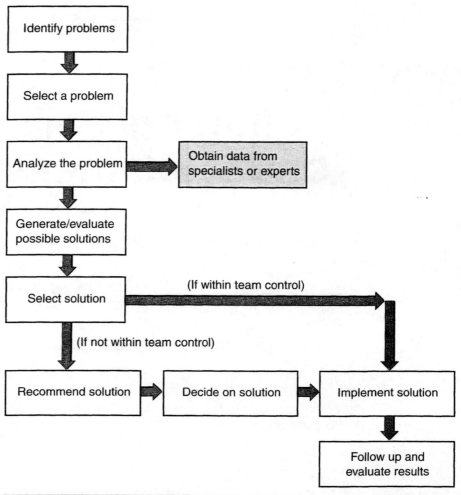

FIGURE 10.1 Problem-Solving Process

political awareness, represents the art of "positive politicking." Refer to the "Problem-Solving Worksheet" on pp. 149–51 as you go through the following steps.

Identify the Problems   This may be the easiest step, because team members, organization members, or community influences are often quick to identify problems for the team. Teams are often formed after a problem has been identified and then given the task of solving that problem. The team must look, however, at the issues that have been identified and then break those issues down to their most fundamental elements. Some questions are: Do the issues identified have a common theme? Are they symptoms of a different, smaller, or bigger problem? The goal of this step is to identify true problems that can be solved.

Select a Problem   Because more than one problem can usually be identified, it is important to deal with a single problem at a time. (The process becomes muddled when teams attempt to solve many problems at once.) In prioritizing problems, the team needs to look at resources like time, money, and energy, and then select the most important problem that can be solved given the resources of the team. The team must ask itself, "What are the risks if this problem is not solved?"

Analyze the Problem   Once the problem has been identified and selected, what information is needed to learn more about the whats, whys, wheres, and whens of it? Teams are often so focused on generating possible solutions that they skip the important, yet often time-consuming, step—obtaining data that flushes out the problem so that it can be analyzed. The quality of information analyzed will determine the quality of the solution and implementation. Teams do not want to be "caught with their pants down" from not doing the homework on the problem. A suggested tool is the "Team Decision-Making Summary Sheet," which can be found on p. 151.

Generate/Evaluate Possible Solutions   Brainstorming is an effective way to generate possible solutions, because it is creative and places no restrictions/conditions on the ideas. The goal of brainstorming is to generate as many solutions as possible. Only after ideas have been generated can they be evaluated. Remember: There are many roads to the same destination. Teams should have more than one viable solution. See Step 5 in the Problem-Solving Worksheet.

Select a Solution   The next task of the team is to select the solutions that are best, then determine whether or not each is within the team's control. The tendency at this stage is to entertain only the solutions that can be implemented by the teams. Teams should determine criteria for the best solution. Examples of criteria include the least expensive solution; the ease of implementing the solution quickly; the degree of solving the problem; and the likelihood of creating new problems. Values may also be placed on the criteria to weight them for a more scientific process.

After selecting a solution, the team should decide whether or not implementation is within their control. If it is, the team should plan and execute the solution, then follow up and evaluate results. If it is not within the team's control, a recommendation of how to implement the solution should be prepared and delivered to decision makers. This recommendation should include the appropriate level of participation for the team in the implementation and evaluation processes.

Recommend Solution   The recommendation may be in the form of a written report and/or presentation to one or more decision makers. This is the stage in which teams draw on their positive politicking skills. The degree to which teams determine and meet needs/agendas directly impacts the extent to which the solution and implementation plan will be well received. A common mistake is for a team to fail to explain how it arrived at a recommended solution. Guiding the stakeholders and decision makers through the team's process often eliminates objections before they arise. A suggested tool is the "Evaluating Options Worksheet" on p. 152.

Decide on Solution   Those who are in control of selecting and implementing a solution will be accountable for the success or failure of the solution. This accountability can cause individuals and teams to be cautious in their decisions. Decisions may be made immediately, or they may be delayed, avoided, or referred to a committee, depending on the level of risk and accountability decision makers feel. There are many factors at work in making decisions: acquired information and facts, feelings, and even intuition. Individuals rely on unique combinations of these and other factors to make decisions. Every decision process is different.

Implement Solution   Many solutions fail because a robust implementation plan is not designed as part of the solution, or because the implementation plan is not executed in a way that minimizes risk to the environment. For example, if a solution is to change software that is essential to business operations at multiple sites, the implementation might be staged by site so that operations do not suffer from the change.

Ongoing evaluation should occur while changes are being made. Checks should include questions such as: Are the changes occurring smoothly, on schedule, within budget?

Follow Up and Evaluate Results At this stage the problem has been identified, selected, and analyzed, and a solution evaluated, selected, and implemented. After an appropriate period of time, a final evaluation should include these questions:

Did we solve the problem?

Are there signs that the problem could reoccur?

Why was the solution successful/unsuccessful?

Do we have any unfinished business regarding this specific problem/solution?

If so, how and to whom do we wish to communicate it?

Reflection

Think of a team decision-making process in which you participated and answer the following questions:

Did we identify the problem, or was it already identified and selected for us? Was the problem clear? Was it accurate?

Did we really analyze the problem, using data and information to support the analysis?

Did we generate and evaluate more than one possible solution?

Was the solution within our control?

Did we facilitate in the implementation and evaluation?

	Problem-Solving Reflection	
Problem-Solving Step	*What We Did Well*	*What We Could Have Done Better*

Obstacles to the Problem-Solving and Decision-Making Processes

In the decision-making process, teams often encounter issues that challenge both the quality of a decision and its acceptance. Particularly problematic to the process are:

Loss of focus

Rush to accomplishment

Rigid mindsets

Intimidating environment

Unwillingness to deal with difficult issues

Domineering and reluctant participants

Process disruptions

LOSS OF FOCUS

Teams often find themselves treading water in the decision-making process. They rehash the same ideas or issues over and over again but have difficulty coming to a resolution. Meetings are characterized by hours of conversation with little progress.

This problem of focus can be addressed in two ways. The first way is to follow the decision-making process consciously, that is, clearly identify the problem or opportunity and reduce it to writing. If necessary, post it in a well-trafficked area so that everyone can see it. Then, deliberately move to the exploration stage and track the ideas and suggestions that come up. Once again, make a deliberate shift to the next stage where alternatives are clear and visible. This logging of specific information and actions is particularly helpful for issues that become complex. Team members need to see how issues are related to each other, what to do next, and what has been accomplished.

The second method of assuring focus is to record in writing the minutes of meetings, highlighting the key issues and decisions made by team members. An ongoing action plan format that lists responsibilities accepted by individual team members is useful to track progress from meeting to meeting. Teams may also find helpful the mindmap described in Chapter 4. Use it both for taking minutes and tracking the decision-making process. The mindmap can be a living document that the team can add to and amend as the decision-making process evolves.

RUSH TO ACCOMPLISHMENT

Teams are often keenly aware of the pressure for them to make timely decisions. Unfortunately, the pressure to act quickly often results in the team engaging in superficial and limiting discussions where fewer alternatives are explored and the quality of decisions is compromised.

The specific liability that a team incurs when it rushes to accomplishment is that of *satisficing,* a coined term derived from the words "satisfied" and "sacrifice," because when a team "satisfices," it stops exploration when the first acceptable alternative comes to the table. As ideas are being discussed, a team member says, "That will work," and if the rest of the team agree, the decision is made. Perhaps better ideas are "sacrificed" at the expense of quickly "satisfying" the issue with a decision.

Again, by deliberately following the problem-solving process, the team is building in a reminder to explore more than one idea. There are several other methods a team can use to prolong and improve the exploration part of decision making. One is the skilled use of dialogue. By continually asking questions around a topic without accepting or rejecting any ideas, the team extends its time to make a decision and is likely to generate more alternatives.

RIGID MINDSETS

Teams are comprised of individuals who have outlooks based upon their past experiences. Team members through self-assessment must check their paradigms for sets of beliefs which are very strong. If a member has experiences and attitudes that create a rigid mindset, others in the team can participate in exercises that challenge assumptions.

INTIMIDATING ENVIRONMENT

Intimidating environments create a climate where team members are reluctant to speak for fear of being verbally attacked. Verbal attacks are characterized by two elements: the use of the word "you" and the presence of negative judgment. Examples of statements that create intimidating environments would include:

"You never listen."

"You only care about your own department."

"Money is all you ever talk about."

"You never come to meetings prepared."

"You are always afraid to try something new."

"You talk just like an accountant."

"You just don't see the big picture."

Statements like these have a negative impact not only on the person speaking but on all members of the team, who usually conclude it is better to remain silent than to risk ridicule.

Ground rules that discourage personal "put downs" and ongoing process assessments of how team members communicate with each other can keep this problem under control. If the person in power is creating the negative environment, it might be useful to bring in an outsider to do a process assessment. If the growth and development of the team is valued, the team should address issues from a team perspective rather than assess individual blame. The truth is that when a team experiences a negative environment, everyone has played a role in creating it and must play a role in repairing the damage.

An exercise that can be used regularly to help every member improve the team process is completing a "Contributor Feedback Worksheet," such as the one following:

Team member name: _____

You make the team more effective when you: _____
_____
_____
_____
_____

The team process would improve if you would do the following: _____
_____
_____
_____

There are many variations for this exercise. The keys to making it effective are:

1. Do the exercise regularly as part of an ongoing improvement process rather than just in response to a problem. Doing the exercise as expected and routine allows people to be less defensive in receiving the feedback.
2. Focus on how to improve the future work of the team so that the feedback does not degenerate into blame.
3. Teach participants to give helpful feedback that focuses on behaviors rather than personalities. Such a focus allows people to be able to use the information and adjust their behavior without feeling attacked. It is easier to change behaviors than personalities.

UNWILLINGNESS TO DEAL WITH DIFFICULT ISSUES

Many teams have sacred cows—issues they are unwilling to discuss. Often these issues are critical to addressing problems at hand. Avoiding discussion of these issues frequently results in the team's rehashing nonsignificant aspects of the problem, thereby never being able to move forward.

Difficult issues need to be addressed in a straightforward but nonthreatening manner. For example, as a regular part of dealing with a new or chronic issue, the team can draw out underlying causes, politics, and emotions that could keep the team from resolving the issues at hand. This information could be gathered either in an open forum, or, if the difficulties are threatening, by using the following feedback form:

Issue: _____

What uncomfortable things do we need to discuss and resolve about this issue before we can begin to address it seriously?

Current mindsets _____

Personal politics _____

Organization history _____

Other _____

Each person completes the form. All forms are collected, and common issues are identified. One by one the team deals with these issues either in an open session or in subgroups that present their recommendations to the entire team.

DOMINEERING AND RELUCTANT PARTICIPANTS

Teams bring together people with many different styles of interaction. At the extreme ends of the interaction continuum you have domineering and reluctant participants. Both are quite common in team situations, and both cause special communication problems for the team.

Domineering participants affect two important resources for teams: time and ideas. When the domineering member monopolizes air time, other members, especially less assertive ones, often conclude that participating is just not worth the effort. The impact of the decision not to participate goes beyond simply not communicating at the meeting. Deprived of input, the team member loses interest in the team and its task and becomes a member in name only.

This leads to the second loss to the team—ideas. Domineering team members prevent other ideas from coming to the table. The team is frustrated and becomes less effective than it could be. It is unlikely that the domineering member has the best ideas all of the time, but even if that person's ideas are good, those ideas represent only one approach. The choice of multiple perspectives is lost.

There are two kinds of domineering team members—positive and negative. If the domineering person is simply talkative and enthusiastic, coaching the person to change his or her verbal behaviors tends to be most effective. Perhaps the most valuable behavior change is to get the person to move from giving information to asking questions of others. Given that the person is generally positive, it is not desirable for the person just to keep quiet, which is probably not possible anyway. Allowing a positive domineering person to play the role of facilitator can be effective as the person focuses his or her energy on getting ideas from others.

The negatively domineering person poses a different sort of problem. This person drives others out, not only by monopolizing airtime but through negative and critical remarks. Tightening up the team's process structure is the best way to handle this person. The team must establish and enforce ground rules on supportive verbal behaviors. These ground rules can be formally enforced by structuring the conversations around the issue, if necessary. A good method for formal structuring for the facilitator is to use a "T" account for recording information on issues. On a white board or flip chart the facilitator makes two columns, representing the positive and negative sides of the issues or recommendation. The facilitator systematically addresses each team member, asking for information to go on both sides of the chart. By collecting information in such a manner, the team gets a holistic view of the issues, and the impact of the domineering person is minimized.

Depending on the culture of the team, there are other informal approaches that can be used to monitor negative verbal behaviors. Some teams give each member a soft sponge ball, and when a team member starts to get negative, someone tosses a ball at him or her. At the end of the meeting, team members discuss the level of negativity in the discussion and how to minimize it. On occasion, a team will assess a fine or punishment (e.g., bring treats to the next meeting) for collecting too many sponge balls. This exercise is best used intermittently to remind teams to keep their discussions on the "can do" track. It is also more effective with a team that is mature enough to use humor effectively. The newer or stressed team is better off using a formal structure such as the "T" account to balance the discussion in the face of domineering participants.

Reluctant participants create a less visible but no less damaging obstacle to effective team participation. A basic tenet of successful teams is that people are members because they have an interest in the team task and something to offer in accomplishing that task. If the participant is not contributing, the underlying cause is usually one of two things: commitment or intimidation. If the person is unprepared or does not seem to care, it is time for the team to discuss team purpose and commitment. Perhaps the team has gotten off track; or maybe the organization politics have changed to make the team task less valuable. It is important for the team not to jump prematurely to the conclusion that it is the team member who is at fault. This is particularly true if the reluctance is a new behavior for the member or if the team as a whole is becoming less participative.

If the reluctance is an individual team member issue, discussion of the roles and responsibilities of team members may help. Team member interest and outside demands often shift over time. The team needs to assess that members and their roles are still appropriate to the task (see the checklist of creative teams roles on p. 153). Successful teams make it possible for a team member to change commitment level or to leave the team without hassle or disgrace. A sign of team maturity is the ability for members to address the internal changes that accompany team evolution.

If the reluctance to participate is caused by intimidation, the team first must look at its process. Is it easy for people to have an opportunity to speak? Is it safe for team members to throw out suggestions? A good evaluation of the team style of participation will help explain why any team member is reluctant to participate. The team can then encourage more participation. Examples of appropriate encouragement might include organized opportunities for input, increased use of supportive verbal behaviors, or action that reduces the importance and influence of power in the group.

PROCESS DISRUPTIONS

It is easy for people to slip into unsupportive verbal habits. Interrupting and engaging in side conversations are two behaviors that frequently occur in team meetings and have a negative impact on the team process. Teams usually use ground rules to prevent these disruptions, but because these habits are so commonplace, the team often has to monitor and reinforce its ground rules.

Interruptions signal an unwillingness on a team member's part to listen to what another team member is saying. Not listening often contributes to an intimidating team environment. Interruptions can be driven by ego, power, or just poor manners, but for the team to be effective, conversation must be relatively free of interruptions.

Increasing awareness is the first step in changing interrupting behavior. Using silence following the interruption, or making a statement recognizing the interruption often makes the speaker aware of his/her actions. From a team perspective, an effective tool to identify and modify this and other verbal behaviors is to videotape or audiotape a meeting. When the video or audiotape is played back, the team can see and hear itself in action. Video is particularly effective because team members can see not only their own behavior, but they can also witness their impact on others.

Team members will be reluctant to use and view the video if it is a source of embarrassment or blame. The key to using video as a feedback tool is to focus on finding examples of useful verbal behaviors. A focus of understanding how the team interacts and of learning new skills will go a long way toward making this highly useful tool a part of the team's continuous improvement effort.

Side conversations are a plague to many meetings. While one person is trying to address the group, two or three other members are engaged in another conversation. Team size can encourage side conversations. As the team grows past ten or twelve members, it becomes difficult for everyone to have adequate airtime. While most people have an interest in what others think, they also have a need for input. Without the opportunity to contribute, the team member may become indifferent or bored. The resulting behavior is often a side conversation.

To avoid side conversations the team first needs a ground rule that sets the expectation for attention to the speaker. After that foundation, effective teams provide means for every member to contribute on a regular basis. Using the verbal behaviors of seeking information and asking questions can assure that everyone has a chance to contribute to the conversation.

Team members should be encouraged to write down the ideas, questions, and related issues that they want to contribute during presentations. Teams may even create their own forms for note taking. This practice encourages organized discussions and provides an expectation that side conversations and interruptions are not valued or necessary.

Reflection

Reflect on a past team that you have observed for some time. Complete the process assessment below to identify the strengths and weaknesses of the team's participation. Note that this assessment may be used in the current team as well.

Process Assessment		
	Strength	*Weakness*
Focus		
Mindsets		
Pace of progress		
Environment		
Participants		
Process disruptions		
Willingness to deal with difficult issues		

Handling Conflict within the Team

While there are a number of things we can do to minimize conflict, there are times when conflict surfaces and must be addressed. Conflict is usually emotionally driven and often involves anger. Whether the conflict is one-on-one or among more than two

Conflict often involves anger.

team members, we can learn to deal positively with our own angry feelings by understanding that their source is almost always a perceived threat.

We can effectively attempt to control ourselves by:

- *Putting the situation in its proper perspective:* Ask ourselves questions such as, Will this matter in a month, a year, ten years? Would this situation seem as important if other people were involved? Must I learn to accept the circumstances, or can they be changed?
- *Examining the best and worst case scenarios:* Often, visualizing the extreme outcomes and realizing that the end result will be better than the worst case scenario keep speculations in check.
- *Examining personal attachment to the outcome:* Ask ourselves questions such as, Will I be embarrassed if the situation doesn't go as I want? Why do I feel so strongly about this?

We can effectively confront the anger of others by:

- *Not allowing it to hook us into conflicts that are none of our business:* Realizing when conflicts are not about us and our positions enables us to pick only the important battles.
- *Recognizing the futility of attempting to dissolve anger through logic:* When there is frustration, it only adds to the conflict. Avoid frustration by remembering that logic may not dissolve the anger.
- *Stating what we feel and want as clearly and pleasantly as possible:* We can do this by focusing on "I" statements rather than "You" statements.
- *Being reasonable but sticking to our principles:* There are times when we do not want to compromise if it will compromise integrity.
- *Ignoring abuse and responding only to reasonable statements:* By communicating in this fashion, we send the message that we are not going to get hooked into an argument or into making negative responses.

We can use the following strategies for communication that involve conflict:

- *Avoid being judgmental:* We can do this by dealing only with present behavior rather than past or potential injustices.
- *Pay attention to the nonverbal content of communication:* Are statements made with open or positive body language?
- *Avoid interpreting motives of others:* Interpretation may more accurately be projection or speculation.
- *Use questions of clarification:* This practice prevents statements from being taken the wrong way.
- *Refrain from giving advice:* "If I were you" statements cause people to become defensive.
- *Summarize points of agreement and disagreement:* This shows a more balanced picture of a situation and avoids focusing only on areas of disagreement.

Occasionally, conflict may escalate to a level where it is appropriate to leave the scene. When disagreements become very emotional, it is important to draw from the following techniques.

- *Attempt to maintain nonthreatening body posture:* This must become a conscious self-check.
- *Never touch a person in an attempt to calm them down:* Touching to some people is a way of communicating power or control.

- *Use distracting questions:* This may help to lessen the escalation temporarily.
- *Speak calmly, firmly, and soothingly:* If we are not sincere, this tone will come across as being patronizing.

Reflection

Think of an example of team conflict that escalated out of control. What techniques were used to bring the situation back to a functional level of communication? Were the techniques helpful, or did they add to the conflict? Why?

Problem-Solving Worksheet

Step 1: Identify the problem

What is happening now? _____

_____

How do you know this is a problem? _____

_____

What is the loss or waste? _____

_____

What are the costs? _____

_____

What do you want to happen? _____

_____

Step 2: List the possible causes of the problem

_____
_____
_____
_____
_____
_____

Step 3: Categorize the causes

Step 4: Generate possible solutions

_____
_____
_____
_____
_____
_____
_____
_____

Define Criteria for a Good Solution   (criteria might include time, cost, resources, career impact, visibility, politics, etc.)

Criteria	Weight
_____	_____
_____	_____
_____	_____
_____	_____
_____	_____

Step 5: Evaluate alternative and decide on solution

Fill in criteria and weight from information developed in Step 4. List each alternative. Then, on a scale from 1 to 10 (with 10 meaning the alternative completely meets the criteria) rate the alternative on each criteria and multiply by its weight. Add the weighted ratings to get the total score. The highest score indicates the most favorable alternative.

Alternative \ *Criteria*	*#1*	*Wt.*	*#2*	*Wt.*	*#3*	*Wt.*	*#4*	*Wt.*	*Total*

Chosen Solution:

_____

Step 6: Develop action plan for resolution

Action to be taken: _____

Plan:

Step	Priority	Preceding Action	Start and Finish Dates	Responsibility	Success Measure	Reward

Team Decision-Making Summary Sheet

Overview of the issue and desired outcome:

_____

Data gathered (issues, costs, perspectives, etc):
-
-
-
-
-
-
Conclusions from data:

_____

Options to consider:
1.

2.

3.

_____

Evaluating Options

1. List the options in the far lefthand column.
2. For each alternative, fill in the boxes as follows:
   - Resolution of Problem.   Enter one of the following words: HIGH (completely resolves problem), MEDIUM (partially resolves problem), or LOW (does not resolve problem).
   - Positive/Negative Impact.   Aside from its effect on resolving the matter at hand, list the various types of positive and negative impact that the alternative might have.
   - Costs.   List the cost associated with the alternative including money, time, materials, etc.
   - Time to Implement.   Indicate how long it would take to implement the alternative.

Criteria for Evaluation

Alternative Solutions	*Resolution of Problem*	*Positive Impact*	*Negative Impact*	*Costs*	*Time*

Reflection

When teams are faced with making course corrections, individual team members must assess their individual positions as well as the positions of other team members in order to formulate a plan to communicate those perspectives.

Describe a problem that needs corrective action:_____
_____
_____

Think about and write your position: _____
_____
_____

Describe the positions of other team members: _____
_____
_____

What words will you use to discuss your position about how to deal with the issue?
_____
_____

Creative Team Roles

Problem solving involves using creativity to identify possible solutions. Creative teams are made up of creative roles. For truly creative efforts, a good mix of roles must be represented in the team.

Generally speaking there are 5 major roles: idea generators, designers, promoters, implementers, and evaluators. Check the following comments that best describe your behaviors in your current team. Note how it is possible to assume different roles according to team requirements.

IDEA GENERATORS

Find new ways to do things

Ask "What if . . ."

Tend to focus only on ideas and concepts

Are result driven

PROMOTERS

Visualize end result

Are optimistic

See links among applications

Provide momentum

Promote ideas

DESIGNERS

See the big picture

Identify resources needed to complete projects

Define performance standards

Define step-by-step procedures

Provide guidance and tools

Insulate team from outside restrictions

IMPLEMENTERS

Are detail-oriented

Tend to follow rules

Work to fill the gap between the generators and promoters

EVALUATORS

Guide projects by clear plans/budgets

Tend to be very definitive in decisions

Insist on maintaining performance standards

Are concerned with productive use of resources

Are concerned with deadlines and policies

Adapted from *What a Great Idea* by Charles "Chic" Thompson.

Reflection

Think of a team that solved a problem using the problem solving process. Did the team structure include all 5 major roles: idea generators, designers, promoters, implementers and evaluators?

CHAPTER

External Politics
and Implementation

Learning from this chapter:

■ To understand the importance of the interests that are external to the team and organization.

■ To explain strategies for influencing and relationship-building skills to further the acceptance of team goals and products.

■ To identify specific skills and attitudes needed to meet external interests.

Other things I want to learn about implementation of team ideas external to the team and organization:

■

■

Purpose

The purpose of this chapter is to emphasize the importance of teams directing their work toward the organization and its external community. Too often teams become islands unto themselves, and their work loses focus. Several external forces impact teams. Organizations have realized that within the various functions there are predictable conflicts such as between production and marketing. Cross-functional teams represent the typical organization's departmental agendas. However, forces such as environmental accountability, technology changes, and legal requirements are examples of external influences that impact a team's work.

External forces often impact teams.

Focus

For a team to be truly effective, it must maintain an external focus. It is very easy for teams to withdraw into themselves. Ironically, the better the team works together, the more often they focus inward. The team works hard, but its results are either not appropriate because it has lost sight of its audience, or are unacceptable because key people were not included in the team decision-making process.

154

Many times teams are disappointed because others do not value the problem to which they propose a solution. Teams need continually to validate their purpose, especially to the external environment.

Teams need to use their sponsors to gather information about what is important to others, where the mine fields are, how to use the organizational systems efficiently, and how to understand history. Because the web of relationships is constantly changing, the process of information gathering cannot stop. Influencing and "socializing an idea" within the organization is a way of communicating the direction a team is going in order to receive feedback along the way. Ideally, by the time a team has successfully completed a project, there should be no surprises or secret unveilings. The organization will have already bought into the ideas being presented and prepared to listen to other ideas for implementation.

Reflection

Think of a specific problem that you addressed as a member of a team. Assign as many perspectives as possible. Were all of the perspectives considered? Was the solution communicated in such a way as to demonstrate that each perspective's needs were considered?

Environment of Change

Teams often expect the outside world to stand still while they are working on their projects. This is especially true of task teams. They are frustrated when their task changes under them. What can the team do to identify changes, address impact, and adjust? The attitude of flexibility and the understanding of ongoing change is a key attribute of successful teams.

Understanding the dynamic nature of organizations is key to making change happen. Since change is going to happen, why not be proactive rather than reactive to the change? Teams can make changes happen by creating a sense of urgency. By simply pointing out the threats inherent in staying the same and the opportunities that exist with change, teams can be prepared for change. Enlisting the help of others is important. Teams should identify those individuals whose opinions can be neutralized and those whose opinions can be changed with information.

Flexibility is the key to dealing with the changing variables that impact teams.

Change is the only constant in organizations. All ground rules and frameworks should be flexible enough to deal with the changing variables that impact teams during the problem-solving process. For instance, a variable that typically changes in organizations is budgeting. Budgeting can change time frames, which in turn may impact the level of commitment that individuals have toward solving a problem. This snowball effect of change makes it difficult for teams to deal with change. The following "Change Response Worksheet" may be used to identify and respond to changes in the environment.

Change Response Worksheet
Team Goal: _____
Team Tasks: _____
Change: _____
Impacts of change on goal: _____

Impacts of change on tasks: _____

Impacts of change on team members: _____

Opportunities presented by change: _____

Liabilities caused by change: _____

Strategy to address change: _____

Goals of Influencing

How do we know that differences exist in perspectives? By comparing like things to like things? What if we don't have like things to compare? After all, people are different, and we can get ourselves into trouble if we make assumptions for the purpose of comparison. The best way to determine differences in perception is to make a sincere effort to learn how and why people see things the way they do.

Without becoming overly analytical, there are some easy strategies for digging in and discovering differences. Always assume that you need to learn more. Make an effort to understand the personal and professional interests people have in situations. Explore how they arrived at their perspective, and perhaps it will give you the opportunity to focus on similarities rather than differences. Ask positive, nonthreatening questions, listen, and ask more questions and more questions.

Team members must talk to each other all the time about everything.

Communication is an ongoing learning process. Practice "lavish communication," which is the practice of talking to people all the time about everything—on the content level and emotional level. Many times we make the mistake of assuming that constituents should be informed of things on a "need to know" basis. The quality of communication and acceptance is poor with this assumption. It's also a good practice to make sure that we only speak for ourselves—not for the interests of others. This practice helps identify more specifically the differences in perspectives.

Once the differences have been identified, attempts can be made to provide information that can reconcile them. When differences are discovered between a team's direction and external influences, there are some key things to remember:

Relationship issues are independent of substantive issues.

Pointing out differences is not usually an attempt to discredit individuals or teams. In the worst scenario, there might be an attempt to sabotage the mission and tasks of a team. These attempts are usually seen for what they are, and not given much attention.

Good relationships are not contingent on agreement. Agreement is nice, but in the most mature self-aware organizational environment, relationships are improved with differences.

Good relationships cannot be "bought" with substantive concessions. In the legal world of quid pro quo, or something-for-something, relationships are compromised, as are the substantive issues.

Relationships must be built on trust, reason, and acceptance. Trust can only be earned through a history of reliability. We should strive to be trustworthy in our relationships and communication. When we withhold information, treat promises lightly, or communicate carelessly, are we being deceptive or dishonest? Some would argue that intent is everything. Failure to communicate completely breeds untrustworthy reputations and relationships.

Constructive attitudes and actions go a long way in creating acceptance. People are diverse, which means that they see things differently. Understand differences rather than try to eliminate them. For personal and professional growth, we must accept individuals personally and deal constructively with those with whom we differ. This does not mean that we must accept their values, perceptions, or conduct, any more than we would try to impose ours upon them. However, when we treat others as equals, we give their interests our attention and the appropriate weight they deserve.

Persuasion and Negotiation Skills

In persuasive communication it is important to view discussions as a means of problem solving and of exploring interests. Most of the time multiple options can be narrowed to a few choices. As choices are limited, the tendency for coercion increases. There is a fine line between persuasion and coercion. Coercion can damage relationships by increasing feelings of rejection and giving rise to a perception of untrustworthiness.

Some of the reasons conflicts occur in organizations are:

Differences in people—different values, intellectual and emotional capacities, and personalities

Limited resources

Communication styles

Unclear job boundaries

Organization complexity

Unclear policies, standards, and rules

Unreasonable deadlines

Collective decision-making process

The Skill of Influencing

The skills needed to engage in positive politicking are called influencing skills. Teams need to learn to identify what they need from others, which things they are willing to compromise, and how to work with others to reach mutual agreements. Without well-developed influencing skills the team is forced to rely on position power, which does not easily build the long-term relationships needed in organizations today.

Successful teams are great at influencing others. This means the team continues to develop skills in the following areas:

Drawing out the needs of others

Developing options that address those needs

Avoiding focus on interests and demands (i.e., final format)

Providing information in a way that others can understand

Finding common ground

Separating principles (needs) and preferences (wants)

Testing expectations against reality

Negotiation Skills

Negotiation skills are an important part of influencing, and they can be developed through awareness and practice. The concepts that negotiation experts deal with in influencing decisions include:

Plan for conflict as much as possible by anticipating perspectives.

Never reject ideas—simply reframe them by asking problem-solving questions.

Challenge the underlying assumptions in your discussion.

Clarify and summarize discussions to minimize misunderstandings.

Deflect attacks and expose tricks, if they are present, by keeping communication-issue oriented.

Know your hot buttons before entering a negotiation arena—like a meeting.

Don't be afraid to buy time to think.

Show trust in your communication and acknowledge individuals.

Let every position "save face" by acknowledging positive aspects.

Offer choices, choices, choices.

Take the ideas of others and build on them in a way that shows the connection.

Use power as little as possible.

Aim for an outcome that represents mutual satisfaction rather than victory/defeat.

Do a post-negotiation assessment. How did you do? What would you do differently?

Teams must work the environment to get needed information, understand the interests of the organization, and build alliances. Without developing good skills and paying attention to external politics, the best ideas will fall on deaf ears and will not be implementable.

We sometimes make the erroneous assumption that team members represent their units. This is a fatal flaw for two reasons:

1. It hinders the team members from working toward the overall purpose of the team and the common good of the organization. The team member feels that he or she must be the advocate for the narrow agenda of the unit he or she represents.
2. It limits the value the team places on getting outside input. Instead of drawing in information from others and seeking validation and contributions along the way, the team assumes that as long as the unit's representative is on the team, whatever solution they set forth will be accepted.

The more closely the team works together, the more likely the team members will stop talking to their constituents as acceptance among the team grows. This can lead to "groupthink," which is something that can occur when team members support each other's ideas because they reinforce their own. Everyone in the team begins to believe the team is on the right track just because they all agree.

Reflection

Consider a meeting or situation where you observed a negotiation that you did not hold an interest in—perhaps a court hearing. Did you find yourself taking a side, or were you able to see both sides? Now think about how you were influenced by the verbal behaviors of the parties. Then evaluate how these behaviors can be used to communicate effectively and influence groups or individuals outside the team.

Emotions and reason must be balanced. There are a lot of personality-assessment instruments that categorize people by traits like Thinkers, Feelers, and so on. Developing an awareness and sensitivity to our own emotions and those of others helps us balance the information and our feelings about it. The questions that follow can assist in developing improved awareness to external political influences.

SELF-ASSESSMENT—POLITICAL SENSITIVITY

Can you identify true power bases?

Do you see motivations and needs of various constituents?

Do you believe that decisions need full commitment?

Are you aware of guarded statements?

Are you solution oriented?

Do you see trusting vs. nontrusting behaviors?

Can you analyze information flows?

Can you identify supportive vs. nonsupportive atmospheres?

Do you regard conflict as natural, even helpful?

Can you separate issues from people?

Do you practice lavish communication?

Can you differentiate approaches and perspectives?

In a meeting, are you aware of seating arrangements, body language, etc.? Are you able to synthesize this information and conduct yourself in a way that will influence?

I need to work on the following to improve my influencing skills:

My development plan:

The Process
of Team Renewal

Learning from this chapter:

■ To identify tools for team evaluation and renewal.

■ To provide connections among concepts introduced in previous chapters.

■ To practice evaluative measures for team activities.

Other things I want to learn about the process of team renewal:

■

■

Purpose

The purpose of this chapter is to give the team the tools for renewal that it needs so that it can continue to grow and be important to the organization's strategic direction.

There is a tie-in with the purpose and process model that emphasizes the ongoing evaluative measures used to sustain the work of the team. These measures are both individual and team oriented, and they allow the team to make transitions. Refer back to Figure II.1 on p. 54.

Under "process," we discussed two important activities for teams: developing both ground rules and effective decision making. However, neither of these activities is a one-time event. Both are ongoing practices or skills that need to be continually monitored, adjusted, and upgraded.

Another process skill that is important to a team is assessment. Teams must build assessment into their regular activities and view it as a development activity rather than one that finds fault. Both "progress toward goals" and "team process" need to be included in the assessment process. As with any assessment, criteria should be consistent with the objectives. Samples of tools are given to suggest formats and common criteria, but teams should adapt them using their own specific criteria. Team objectives change, which is why members must periodically evaluate their structure, process, and flexibility in dealing with internal and external political influences.

There are five guidelines for measuring the work of teams. It is important to look at all five to get an accurate picture of work performance. Measuring only one guideline would result in an unbalanced assessment.

Quantity of team work	Is the team making progress toward its goals? Are team meetings efficient?
Quality of team work	Is the work of the team based on relevant data and information? Are all perspectives considered in developing solutions and making decisions? Are team ideas truly innovative? Does the team have an external focus?
Team knowledge	Is the team learning the skills needed to accomplish its task? Has each person developed as a result of being a member of the team? Does the team have a learning program? Has the team developed a learning culture?
Initiative	Does the team use an effective method for decision making? Do team members do equivalent amounts of "real" work?
Collaboration	Does the team follow its own ground rules? Has the team developed a performance culture?

The initial work of the team includes goal setting as a part of establishing the team's charter.

Teams invariably work under time pressure, and meeting milestones and goals are key measures of the effectiveness of the team. To meet is not enough; the team must show that it is accomplishing what it was chartered to do. This seems obvious, but many teams fall into the trap of thinking they are making progress simply because they keep meeting. By using **quantity of work** measures, the team can hold itself accountable for getting work done.

In addition to moving ahead on its tasks, the team must challenge the quality of its work. This is difficult, because it is hard to be objective about one's own work. Measuring the **quality of work** of the team probably requires the team to do an external reality check with the constituents who must use the outcome of the team's activity.

Learning is a hallmark of an effective team. It is important to understand that the team must gain new skills, both task-oriented skills such as data collection and interpretation, and process-oriented skills such as thinking and evaluating. The team must continually assess where it is gaining **knowledge** on both group and individual levels. Learning assumes a desire for continuous improvement.

Initiative measures assess whether or not the team is taking on challenging tasks and issues. The presence of a risk-taking attitude toward practices is an indication of initiative. Teams can assess themselves and be assessed by external constituents by asking the following questions: Does the decision-making process of the team consider new ideas and challenge the current assumptions, or is it a safe discussion likely to reach solutions similar to current practice? Are members of the team engaged in their work? Do they have a commitment to performance? Are they creative and unassuming in their problem-solving discussions?

Teams can quickly fall apart if the process they use does not value both the people and their time commitments. Teams usually recognize this potential pitfall as they set up their ground rules, but they can easily slip back into poor process habits. **Collaboration** assessment lets the team check how well it is working.

These guidelines are meant to be starting points. As discussed early in the book, each team is unique. It will have specific tasks, ground rules, culture, and external expectations that have to be monitored. The essential aspect of assessment is that it must be done on a regular basis. The more measurement is made to be a part of how the team does business, the less the team will generate defensiveness and the easier it will be for the team to correct its course. If the team waits until an external force identifies a need for corrective action, the necessary changes will be difficult indeed. The "Team Development Assessment" on p. 164 will guide the team in this process.

Measuring performance is only the first part of an assessment process. Performance information must be fed back to team members so that work can be adjusted. How information is fed back to the team is critical to the team's ability to accept and use the information.

Reflection

Think about a situation when you were on a team that did not assess on a regular basis. Identify the problems that festered, such as loss of interest. How would the outcomes have differed if ongoing evaluation had been part of the process?

One of the greatest contributions that Edward Deming made in his work on quality management was to make the employee responsible for his/her own performance measurement. He reasoned that if the person understood how she or he was doing, she or he would take steps to correct or improve. Most of the time in organizations performance information is sent "upstairs," and the people who were evaluated and could use the information to understand their performance never see it. Deming insisted that measurement should be collected by the worker and be useful to the worker. We need to apply this same principle to team performance. Teams will feel empowered when they are given the feedback necessary to make corrections in their courses.

The team itself needs to determine what it considers good performance and create the appropriate measures to evaluate that performance by revisiting the five guidelines for measuring work: quantity of teamwork; quality of teamwork; team knowledge; initiative; and collaboration. The team itself needs to monitor its performance on a regular basis. Again, to borrow from Deming, the purpose of the measure is to provide information to the performer so that he or she can self-correct. Thus the measure becomes developmental and not punitive.

Reflection

Think of individual performance appraisals that you have had in the past. Was the appraisal scheduled—as in annual, semi-annual? Then think about how different the process would have been if your performance feedback had been more regular.

In order for measures to be developmental they must be established at the time of goal setting. When the team decides what it wants to accomplish and how it wants to operate, it must create a way to track whether it is successful in meeting the goals it sets. If the team waits until there is a problem, any attempt at measuring will be viewed as blaming.

Regular assessment of team progress is important to success.

The team needs to set up a measurement process as a part of its team charter. It needs to determine what the indicators of success and progress will be; how those indicators will be measured; and when measurement will occur. In addition, the team needs to decide what to do with the information gathered and how to feed that information back to the team. Quarterly reviews and in-depth annual reviews are recommended, as well as specific problem-driven reviews. Team members must commit to this kind of regular assessment if it is to be beneficial.

Without feedback, the information is useless. Sometimes the measures are apparent, as when deadlines are missed. In the case of a missed deadline, teams may address what to do about the missed deadline. However, teams must ask themselves what kind of information is needed in order to know why the deadline was missed; only then is there any assurance that another deadline will not be missed. This process revisits the need for a learning culture. How can a team uncover this information and understand it without creating defensiveness among its members? How can the team identify earlier warning signals so that it does not have to wait until a deadline is missed to make changes in its behavior? These questions speak to the true power of measurement, and they should be the focus of performance feedback.

Process measures for the team are usually more complex than task measures. Teams are often reluctant to do any process measures at all. Both are necessary to quality team performance. Once measures have been taken, the team faces a dilemma: How do we use the information well created?

Feedback Rules

There are some feedback rules that will help a team accept and use information.

FOCUS ON THE FUTURE

No one can change what he or she did or didn't do in the past. By talking about what went wrong, people become defensive and feel that they have to justify their past actions. That kind of discussion is nonproductive in terms of keeping the problem from occurring again. It doesn't change the current course of action. Instead, it fosters resistance to change. Remember, no one has made a mistake tomorrow. By focusing on the future, feedback allows individuals to benefit from learning while maintaining personal dignity.

FOCUS ON SPECIFICS

Avoid general assessments about team performance, such as "disorganized," "unfocused," or "on track." These terms mean different things to different people. The terms do not help the team understand what to do differently or what behaviors to repeat. A review of both problems and successes should be specific enough to identify the future course of action. This is especially true of successes. In general, if teams make assessments, they focus on recrimination—rather than on what went well so that they can keep doing these things. Here's the principle: If you know what you did wrong, you still need to figure out what to do right. If you know what you did well, you just have to do it again and again. People and teams inherently want to succeed.

FOCUS ON LEARNING

As the team assesses its progress, it needs to match its performance with the organization's needs. Rather than focus on what its deficiencies might be, it needs to identify specifically what it needs to be able to do as a team. This draws the assessment full circle to focus on the purpose of the team. Focusing feedback of negative information on the learning needs of the team provides incentive to change. If feedback simply identifies deficiencies, team members are likely to attribute those deficiencies to individual team members or circumstances, and to miss important opportunities for the entire team to grow.

Reflection

Consider a situation where you received team feedback. Was the team able to use the information?

Was there a focus on the future?

Was there a focus on specifics?

Was there a focus on learning?

Now consider your current team. Has the team received feedback? Was the information useful for course correction? How could feedback be more useful in the future?

Team Development Assessment

This form should be completed by individual team members on a regular basis to rate team progress. The forms should then be discussed by all team members.

Purpose

1	2	3	4	5

Purpose is clear.   Purpose is unclear.

Accountability

1	2	3	4	5

Team members are accountable.   Team members are not accountable.

Ground Rules

1	2	3	4	5

Ground rules are followed.   Ground rules are not followed.

Progress

1	2	3	4	5

Appropriate progress is being made.   Appropriate progress is not being made.

Feelings (inclusion vs. exclusion, commitment vs. noncommitment, loyalty vs. lack of loyalty, pride vs. embarrassment, trust vs. mistrust; see list following):

_____

_____

_____

_____

"FEELINGS" OF EFFECTIVE WORK TEAMS

INCLUSION
- Team members get information that affects their jobs and their lives in the organization.
- New ideas are encouraged and treated with respect.
- Team members receive quick responses from other team members when they ask for help.

COMMITMENT
- Team members make personal sacrifices to make sure the team succeeds.
- Team members care about team results.
- Team members are determined to succeed.

LOYALTY
- Team members go out of their way to ensure the success of their peers.
- Team members give their colleagues the benefit of the doubt when they have apparently failed to fulfill a commitment.

PRIDE
- Feedback is sought out and taken seriously as a chance to improve.
- Team members believe that what they do is important and tied to organization goals.
- Team members have a strong orientation toward the future and expect to exceed their own current levels of performance.

TRUST
- Team members do what they say they are going to do.
- Team members never conceal information from one another.
- Team members are willing to listen to one another and defer to one another because they expect reliable information and good ideas from one another.
- Team members view one another as having the knowledge and skills to perform.

Team Development Survey

Instructions: Using the numbers on the continuum below, select the number that best describes the team for all of the areas.

Don't Know	1	2	3	4	5	6	7	8	9	10
N/A for internal		Never				Sometimes				Always

Team Structure
_____ Goals are clearly stated and flexible.
_____ Initiating, planning, executing, and evaluating are shared by the team.
_____ The team is self-motivated.
_____ The skills of individual team members are suited to the task.

Team Climate
_____ Team members feel a sense of unity and cohesion.
_____ Team members express themselves freely but consider the welfare of the whole team.
_____ Responsibilities are shared.
_____ Team leadership is shared among members at different times.

Team Process
_____ Progress toward goals can be seen.
_____ The team follows a problem-solving process.
_____ The team performs regular self-checks.

Team Politics
_____ The team maintains an external focus.
_____ The team is growing in its ability to identify and meet the needs of constituents.
_____ Team members understand the importance of conflict in teams and organizations.
_____ The team is growing in the skills of influencing, persuasion, negotiation, and conflict resolution.

Team Effectiveness Review

Things I like about this team:

1.
2.
3.
4.
5.
6.

Things I do not like about this team:

1.
2.
3.
4.
5.
6.

Action Steps

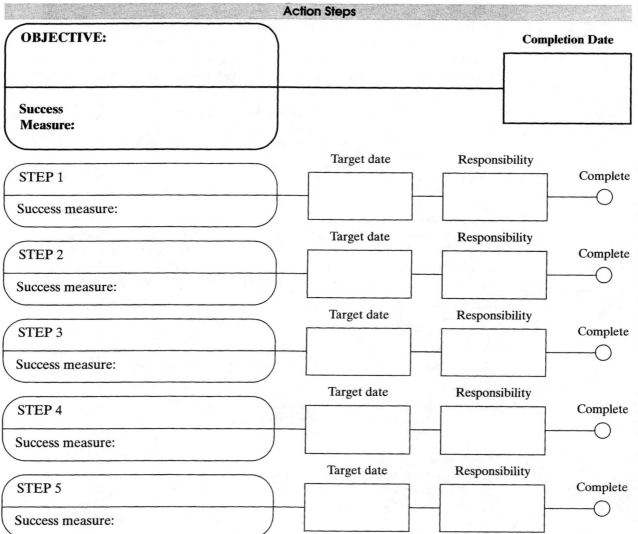

Conclusion

The Future of Teams

The process of completing the exercises of this text is designed to lead to a holistic view of teams. While we discuss it in terms of structure, climate, process, and politics, these elements are fluid and concurrent. In the future, teams will be more common, less structured, and larger. Unless organizations can find another mechanism where people from different functions can meet and quickly make decisions, teams are here to stay. However, teams need to match the demands of the future and not the past. They need to be more spontaneous and do a better job of demonstrating problem resolution.

Organizational structures will change to use teams as a primary function. Organizational charts will be redesigned to show multiple functions and processes. As organizations experience more success and become comfortable with teams, they will become the structure of choice rather than the structure of force. This will cause a redefinition of "affliliation" within the organization and open up a wealth of human resources. Redefinition includes the use of more "virtual teams" with members who are loaned from parts of organizations all over the world. Technology facilitates the increased use of this forum to solve problems, make decisions, and implement change. The benefits of virtual teams have proven to empower teams and organizations.

One of the biggest criticisms of teams has been the time it takes to develop a team. Organizations must find ways to speed up the process. When teams are truly embraced by the organization, the process becomes less of a drain on resources. Teams can be a core competency for organizations. We must accept the fact that we will learn as we go and make mistakes. By abandoning the ideal of perfection, we free ourselves to enjoy the process—mistakes and all. It is the mistakes that take us back to the beginning of the continuum to enjoy the improved process again and again. It is also the mistakes that enable us to better appreciate imperfect people and imperfect processes everywhere.

End of Section Activities

Discussion Questions

How can teams focus on problem solving, internal and external influences, and the many other considerations at the same time?

1. Discuss the place of renewal in the team process.
2. Discuss the criticisms of using the problem-solving/decision-making model.
3. Review the importance of ongoing assessment.

Application: Critical Incidents

1. You are part of a design team that is assigned the task of designing, developing, and implementing a new employee orientation program. The timeframe is short, and many team members have limited participation due to other work.

The leader of the team has strong feelings and opinions about the scope of the project. Other team members are too busy with other responsibilities to assume much responsibility; however, you believe that the scope is based upon the wrong assumptions, and you suggest performing a study to validate the needs of new employees.

Your suggestion challenges the leader, who tells you to either commit to the existing course of action or resign from the team. Given these circumstances, characterize the politics in terms of internal influences.

2. You are a software sales representative for a market-dominating company. Your regional manager selects you to be part of a cross-functional team that will provide feedback to an implementation team for a new product line. You will represent the sales rep's view on this team and will hear the views

of engineers, programmers, accountants, trainers, help-desk employees, and so forth.

This appears to be an effort to anticipate internal constituent needs. However, after the introduction of the new product line, it is clear that it is being launched too soon without proper testing.

What dialogue can you use in this situation?

Background Reading

Many of the concepts in this section are supported by research and other writings. Some of the key foundation work is included in the materials below. If you want to expand your knowledge of team politics, negotiation, and persuasion techniques, please explore this information.

Dimock, Hedley G. 1987. *Groups: Leadership and Group Development.* San Diego, CA: University Associates. A practical and theoretical approach to roles within groups.

Fischer, Roger, and Scott Brown. 1988. *Getting Together.* New York: Penguin Books. A discussion on the obstacles that occur in teams.

Goodstein, L. D., and J. W. Pfeiffer. 1974. *A Handbook of Structured Experiences for Human Relations Training.* Vol. 3, rev. San Diego, CA: University Associates. A good resource for sample instruments and simulations for teams.

Katzenbach, Jon R., and Douglas K. Smith. 1993. *The Wisdom of Teams.* Boston, MA: Harvard Business School Press. An excellent foundation for team theory.

Individual Team Charter

Structure

MEMBERSHIP

Strengths of current team design:

Ways to capitalize on strengths:

Ways to improve on design:

SKILL MIX

Skills well-represented on team:

Skills to develop:

Skills to find for team to use:

PURPOSE

Team purpose: _____

Major goals:

Goal	Milestone	Milestone	Milestone	Milestone

Decision-making authority: _____

_____

Relationship to sponsor: _____

_____

RESOURCES AVAILABLE:

Experts _____

Support people _____

Financial _____

Technical _____

Facility _____

Other _____

Other _____

ASSUMPTIONS

Assumptions around teamwork:

Assumptions around team task:

Assumptions that need to be challenged:

MEASURES OF SUCCESS

Key Goal	*Indicator for Success*	*Indicator for Concern*

PROCESS FOR COLLECTING INFORMATION

_____

_____

_____

LEADERSHIP

Who plays leadership roles? External _____

Internal _____

How will leadership be carried out in team?_____

_____

_____

LEADERSHIP DEVELOPMENT

Team leadership strength to capitalize on:	*Team leadership development need:*

Process

Ground Rules	
Length of meetings	
Tardiness	
Absence	
Level of "being there" at meetings	
Substitution for absent member	
Getting information from absent member	
Getting information to absent member	
Quality of work expected	
Quantity of work expected	
Timeliness of assigned work	
Confidentiality	
Other	
Other	
Ground rule enforcement	

Contributor Skills			
Skills	*Importance*	*Expectations*	*How to Develop*
Initiate			
Energize			
Organize			
Build relationships			
Learn			
Embrace change			

Culture

Commitment Levels		
Team Member	*Commitment to Give*	*Responsibilities*

TRUST

Ways to develop:

-
-
-
-
-

RITUALS

For entering team members:

For exiting team members:

For celebration:

DIVERSITY

Team Profile		
Dimensions	*Similarities*	*Differences*
Culture		
Experience		
Thinking Style		

CREATIVITY

Techniques to focus on:

-

-

-

-

Politics

EXTERNAL FOCUS

People to involve:

-
-
-

Perspectives to consider:

-
-
-

RENEWAL

Repeat Team Effectiveness Review.

Index